God's Emergency Room

WHY DOES LIFE HURT? SO MUCH!

By:

Kim Bernasconi

WestBow
PRESS
A DIVISION OF THOMAS NELSON

ISBN: 978-1-4497-5811-0 (sc)
ISBN: 978-1-4497-5812-7 (e)

Library of Congress Control Number: 2012913965

WestBow Press books may be ordered through booksellers or by contacting:

WestBow Press
A Division of Thomas Nelson
1663 Liberty Drive
Bloomington, IN 47403
www.westbowpress.com
1-(866) 928-1240

Because of the dynamic nature of the Internet, any web addresses or links contained in this book may have changed since publication and may no longer be valid. The views expressed in this work are solely those of the author and do not necessarily reflect the views of the publisher, and the publisher hereby disclaims any responsibility for them.

Any people depicted in stock imagery provided by Thinkstock are models, and such images are being used for illustrative purposes only.

Certain stock imagery © Thinkstock.

Printed in the United States of America

WestBow Press rev. date: 08/01/2012

DEDICATION:

"God's Emergency Room" belongs to God. It is not mine to dedicate He is the originator. I am only a vessel that He has used to help others like me. So let me say that it is dedicated to all of those that read it and I pray you feel the love and strength God will give you as you read on.

I would like to thank my brother and sister-in-law, Michael and Dottie Bernasconi for their persistent unconditional love, believe and support in me, even when I felt that I was not worthy to share God's words.

Contents

PREFACE

"GOD'S EMERGENCY ROOM", "Why Does Life Hurt? So Much!" is a small part of my testimony on how I thought God did everything bad to me in my life and nothing good for me. Whether you feel the same way as I use to or not has no bearing on what can be revealed to you in the ongoing series of "GOD'S EMERGENCY ROOM". I am going to attempt the challenge to gently show you the way to the truth about life's burdens and joy, by showing you and myself that my beliefs that God and the Bible has nothing to do with the answers to today's pains and struggles is not reality and that: **I was DEAD wrong!**

"I never promised you a rose garden." Is a quote that I heard my whole life and let me tell you it annoyed me to no end, even I was smart enough to realize that a rose garden is full of painful thorns.

How could I get through those thorns and endure the pain of them without pertection and why would I want to go through anything so painful to get to beauty?

My testimony through the words and love of God will show you how to get through the thorns in the garden of life with his love and get you into the beauty and graces of the Lord. With and open heart and mind you can become very aware of why you are here on earth and who put you here.

The series of God's Emergency Room was not my idea, there is no way this human body named Kim would have voluntarily become a believer of The Lord Jesus Christ. God had other plans for me though and this long journey was not going to be easy for me or Him in the beginning, But-

Matthew 19:26 With God all things are possible.

I was so full of what God and the Bible was not, that my head and heart was locked up as tight as a vault to anything I could not control, touch or prove. God asks only that you try to identify with my testimonies and read with an open mind. I will not lie to you, sharing all my testimony throughout this series with such honesty and humility was not easy for me in my flesh and without the Lord it would never be possible. We will take a rollercoaster ride together through anxiety, panic, marriages, divorces, adultery, breast cancer, gambling, drugs, alcohol, and many other twist and turns.

<u>**Because you are reading this, God is already trying to get your attention**</u>

THE DIS-EASE

*M*y casual friends, acquaintances, or anyone meeting me for the first time would have had absolutely no idea of the secret **turmoil** that was **castrating** my ability to truly **enjoy** anything in **life.** I was truly living by the old quote, "life is a stage" and I deserved an academy award for my day to day acting skills.

"What circumstances in my life would leave me in such **despair**?

That is the question I spent the first fifty-two years of my life unknowingly trying to find the answer to. I held only two positions in the circumstances that showed themselves in my life. The first was that I considered myself to always be the **victim.** I was either the victim of someone and their doings or I was the victim to whatever circumstance that went wrong in my life.

I continuously refused to take any responsibility for my part in the horror shows that cropped up in my life. I also swore that I was being victimized by **God!** This way of thinking that God would victimize me in any way was of course absurd. Due to the fact that I never even acknowledged that there was a God, or at least that he played any part in my life at all. My thinking that God was in control of the bad things in my life, when I refused to acknowledge him for any good that happened in my life reminds me of the following parable.

Some young children find security in having a little imaginary friend. The child uses this imaginary friend for fun, fellowship, love, and whatever other immediate need they want to fill. Although the child cannot see the friend in the physical sense they truly believe and feel the feelings they derive from their experiences together.

Now watch what the same child does when they are caught doing something wrong and they are asked about it by their parents. What do they do? They immediately throw their imaginary friend under the bus.

"I guess I had a whole lot of imaginary friends in my life!"

On the occasions when the feelings of **pleasure and happiness** showed themselves in my or anyone else's world, did I give God the credit? No, I had been the heroic one and I would have sat in the front row at the awards banquet to except my trophy for those good deeds I believed I had accomplished. That you could have bet on! I was inflicted with the false notion that I was always the **hero** and the one that hit the ball out of the park each time, with no help from anyone or anything, least of all God.

Are you already recognizing that I thought everything was about me? Good for you if you have, because I hadn't!

I want to give you some examples of my **ignorance** to the **truths** about this life on earth, and how my lack of **knowledge** to the real truths in life made me feel the way I did in the statements above. I do this in hopes of helping you to understanding how a **heart** empty of **faith** and **The Holy Spirit**, cannot experience, feel, or understand anything with **clarity** or **honest** thoughts, actions, and emotions.

I pray that those of you who are reading my testimony will come to understand that the most important **factor** for me or anyone in the **equation** of sharing their story is that they stay very **transparent** and honest. It is not easy to share about all of my **character defects**, **rebellion**, **confusion** and the huge **mistakes** that I have made. But if I am not both transparent and honest, neither you nor I will find the X- factor in the conclusion to life and death.

Your part in the equation is to do your best not to **compare** the circumstances in my life with the circumstances in your life. That would impede your chance of understanding the pain and confusion in life circumstances and you like I will stay confused and lost.

So do not say to yourself the following.

"Wow, her life was harder than mine!" or "Her life was not as bad as mine!"

Instead let your heart be able to identify with the feelings involved, and the lack of knowledge of the true reasons for these feelings. It is not the intent of these writings for you to waste one second feeling positive or negative feelings about me or my turmoil's in life. Maybe for the first time in a long time this is all about you! Do not allow fear, judgment, or any other negative emotion in your heart or head. That is Satan getting what he wants from you all over again.

Please do not sabotage your chance of finding your way to how and why we are put here on this earth. Find the truth on earth and live with a joy that only the truth can give you, all other comforts are just one of your imaginary friends. I pray that you will open your heart and ears and allow God to speak through me. If you will simply do that and only that for the moment, you will start to receive the graces that he has gifted to me. His gifts are plentiful and just waiting for you to open them.

Pay close attention to the underlined words. They may be the **unknown variable** in the equation of life now. But they do not have to continue to be the unknown. We have all been able to identify with these words at least once in our life and if you do not have an understanding of the word itself and what it means to your life and its situations, you will never open the true gift of life that your creator has given you.

I found in writing this that I really did not know what many of these underlined words' original definitions were in the world's dictionary, and I considered myself quite knowledgeable. I most definitely did not know what they meant to the truth of life or how to deal with or use them. Please, just continue to read and take this journey with me, and do your best to be as honest as you possibly can with yourself. I know that is not an easy thing to do and you may be **scared**, I know I was. But do not be afraid to be honest about all that you are and are not. God already knows everything. There are no **secrets** between you and God whether you believe that or not. He sees and knows all and all he wants from you at this point is for you to come forth and be willing to learn. He wants that revelation to start right here, right now!

He wants you, JUST AS YOU ARE!

I also pray that those of you that have been given the gift of faith (not religion) and have not had to take the same route as those like me in life, to open your heart and understand those of us that could not understand or embrace the love of God either because of our misconceptions, fear of being beaten up by others with the Bible or own ignorance. Just remember you may be the one that God wants to use as a **vessel** to save a **sinner** just like me.

To my new friends, do not let the word sinner that I just used heat up your fire of fear and anxiety. Just chill about it for now, you will understand in time that this word no longer has to be the boogey man.

As I started to look into my life and its events, I realized I had made the choices to take the first steps into most of the turmoil that showed itself in my life. I may not have recognized it at the time, but that first step always affected the outcome of many other life choices to come.

I like to picture it like this. Think of life as a train, the engine is whatever powers up your life and is fueled by whatever substance you put in it. The engine in the beginning is setting on the tracks waiting for the engineer that knows how to move it forward and get it from one place to the other.

Now I needed to add one car to that train for every year of my life. So if I am honest I had fifty two cars connected to that engine. That is a good number of cars, and each one of them was packed to capacity with the treasures and junk of my doings in life so far. Unfortunately, most of them were full of my life's junk, and the people that were willingly or unwillingly involved in my life's calamities. Think of that train and the tons of heavy artillery in it speeding down the tracks. Continuing to pick up out of control speed every day of every year and never stopping for maintenance. Top that off with me being the engineer of that mess and being in control of that deadly weapon, even though I had no idea what made it run or where I was guiding it.

For this testimonial workbook I want you to stay with that picture and take the tour of the egocentric, and prideful, choices I made that put me, and all those involved in the devastating fear of what was coming next.

The first baggage loaded on car number one was the bitter angry divorce of my parents around the age of twelve.

Parents please come to the same revelation I had to accept for my children from my divorces. There are no bomb shelters strong enough to withstand the poisons of the toxic bombs we shoot off at our mates (the mother or father of our children) that can protect our children from future sickness. Whether it be because of divorce or one parent just plain abandoning their children.

Shortly after the finality of the divorce and the loss of my security of having two parents to love and protect me I added another load of baggage to my train. I became a teenage alcoholic and I had the perfect excuse. I was a victim of my parents' divorce. Yes, the divorce was a **devastating** time for all involved, but the reality is that at the age of twelve I would never have become an alcoholic if I had not put the bottle to my lips and ingested it. What was lacking inside me at the age of twelve that made me instinctively think that alcohol could or would answer anything for me or relieve my pain. I will tell you what, monkey see, monkey do.

I knew that it was forbidden by my parents for me to drink this substance even though it was never discussed. But it had an attraction that enticed me, and I had no idea why. I had observed many adults drink this beverage and go from solemn to joy and extreme happiness. The decision to take that first gulp of the forbidden fruit reminds me now of a story that had been read to me when I was a very young girl. This story was the story of Adam and Eve. It was read to me out of a children's Bible story book and that is exactly what I thought it was a fictional bedtime story!

The true meaning of Adam and Eve's choice to eat the fruit from that forbidden tree never registered to me. Again it was just a STORY, it meant no more to me than the big bad wolf in "Little Red Riding Hood" or the cute little story "Goldilocks and the Three Little Bears.

Why was that?

Today I would say that it was because the meaning and truth of that story was never translated to me in a way that I could identify it to my life and my choices. I cannot say that a true understanding of that piece of history would have changed my choices, but I may have connected the two.

Was I not like Eve at that moment when I was being told by the unidentifiable evil serpent that I was being deprived by my father something that he had and enjoyed. In Eve's case she had everything that she needed available to her in the garden except the one tree in the middle of the garden was off limits. She was warned by God that if she touched that tree she would surely die. The serpent (Satan) however spun the command around and deceived her into believing the true reason she was not to touch the tree was because it would give her all that God had. Eve believed the serpent and convinced Adam to also take a bite of the apple from that tree. Did God kill them physically? NO! But both Adam and Eve where banished from the Garden of Eden and they died spiritually. That was the beginning of the flesh and its sin nature that we struggle with and all that goes with it.

Was it not the same for me?

I was not equipped with the tools to know any other avenue that would help stop the pain and lack of security inside of me. But something was convincing me that the forbidden was the answer and the moment I swallowed my first few gulps I felt the warmth and courage flowing down my throat to my stomach. I was in love. It falsely made me feel indestructible. I had found my strength and security. I know now why mind altering, false courage giving, substances are forbidden to young immature minds. I had just caused the death of my maturity and started on the long road of being owned by something that had no right to my love or soul. Whatever it may be, that has you, a friend, or a loved one handcuffed to it will **seduce** you into captivity.

Many things certainly seduced me into captivity throughout my life. There is an invisible line that we all may cross with any worldly thing that makes us feel good. Some of those false securities include, but are not limited to, alcohol, food, drugs, sex, money, work, porn and on and on. I never knew about that invisible line, but when I crossed it my needs and wants turned into the hand cuffs that shackled me from the **freedom** to live a free full **life of truth.** For your sake, do not pretend that you cannot pick at least one thing or person in your life that has tied up your emotions, and makes you believe that it is more important than anything else in the world because it gives you comfort. Or that it is the only way you can handle and enjoy life.

Do not let this be one of the times that I talked about earlier by not being honest with your-self. If you have to control something in your life, it is out of control already. I also came to realize that not all good things we do are good in the long run, such as exercise, dieting, and serving others constantly, if anything is overdone and owns your heart it is bad for you. You are its prisoner!

Marriages and divorces were another area in my life that I always thought I was the victim. All the men I attracted were professional conmen in our marriage situations. The reason I say that is the men I picked were not honest about who or what they represented themselves to be. Nor did they follow through with the promises they had made to me in the **fantasy** state of the relationship.

But you know what? Neither did I!

I will divulge to you that my first marriage took place at the age of seventeen. Again like the alcohol I had made a major decision before the legal, moral and emotional age of maturity. This decision was made so that I could escape the **guidance** of my **parents**. No I was not with child, thank the Lord, but I wanted to feel free. Little did I know the real gift of freedom was something I knew nothing about and this action was not going to free me from anything or anyone. In fact my prison room was going to get even smaller.

Until now at the age of fifty-five I would add the baggage of six marriages to my out of control train. The honest and real problem with these marriages was that I did not give myself and these men the time for us to get to know each other. Because of our hurry and hunger for whatever we thought marriage would give us, we had no idea if we were even compatible for the **sanctity** of **marriage**. What does that mean, sanctity of marriage? Shoot I didn't know, and I didn't even care to consider it.

All things had to be immediate for me. I was always looking for an immediate relief from my emotional pain and to feel that infamous emotional high, which was as fake as a bad Luis Vuitton handbag copy. I hated the flat feeling life gave me. I only knew I was alive when I was feeling the peaks and valleys of life.

The best example I have to explain how I only felt alive when I was experiencing the peaks and valleys of life is to compare it to a heart monitor in the hospital. When you follow the line that monitors the rate and strength of the heart beating, it is either at a peak or valley when the heart is pumping. If the line on the monitor goes in a straight horizontal position across the screen, your heart and life has stopped either temporally, or for infinity. When the line of life was straight and, emotionally flat my life stopped because I had no stimulus and I hated silence. Peace of mind was my enemy and because I was not familiar or comfortable with it, you could bet your life on the fact, I would resuscitate the chaos in lighting speed.

There were times that I would be gifted with the good feelings in life that I constantly searched out for. But each time the **gratification** from them was only **temporary**. The ramifications at the end of these acts, that gave me that false high where always very costly for me. They were costly in different ways, including financially, emotionally, physically, and even if I would not acknowledge it, morally also. The ramifications were also devastating for all of those that surrounded me, and many people that I did not even realize existed on this earth.

My **challenges** in life were many. Some of which I got myself into through making the wrong choices, some out of immature ignorance, others out of outside pressures, and some out of just plain **selfishness** or **rebellion.** But you would have had to pity the poor soul that tried to tell me this about myself.

One of my other down falls was trying to do life on life's terms, according to the world's way of thinking with no want or acceptance of **guidance** from anyone or anything. There are not many people out there that I cannot identify with when it comes to life's stumbling blocks, pathways or bad choices and the repercussions of them. I am also well aware of the fact that there are many of you that are reading this and are unwillingly identifying with me.

So far I have already told you about how I felt like a victim to alcohol, the divorce of my parents, and my own multiple marriages. The list includes but is not limited to rape, unfaithful husbands, premature birth of a son, alcoholic husband, being a single mother, signing over custody of my son, that I loved more than life itself to his father, alienating parts of my family in an unhealthy, and ungodly way, child molestation and living every day of my life with the evil serpent of **anxiety and or panic.**

What came first the chicken or the egg?

What came first the debilitating anxiety and panic, or my wrong choices?

Through all of these situations I was very comfortable in the position of being the victim. That way I never had to take any **responsibility** for my part in the choices I made, or situations I got myself into. I am in <u>no way</u> excusing the **evil** part that other people may take in our life tragedies and wrong doings. God knows who they are and what they have done. Unfortunately, the reality is that there is evil out there in this world and it is always looking for his next pray. But I needed to take a look at some of the decisions I made that opened the door of opportunity for evil to come into my life, willingly or not.

I was always afraid of the unidentified "boogeyman" that always wanted to get me. However I kept inviting him in, without knowing who he was. That unidentified boogeyman was going to be given a name in my future, but more importantly I was going to understand that I did not have to fear him any longer.

The other fact that I needed to begin to realize is that not everything that happens in life is happening directly to me. I did not know that I was not the **axis of the earth** and everything in it or on it.

What is? I had no idea.

My life was a constant battle to do the right thing. The right thing according to who or what, I do not know. Or I was trying to cover up the wrong things I had already done. It was a constant battle that quickly turned into a vicious cycle. I need for all of you that are reading this to understand that nothing I was doing or experiencing was that much out of the ordinary according to this **morally** challenged world of ours.

I had some good things happen in my life. I got sober from alcohol at the age of thirty. I had a wonderful son and gave birth to a daughter in sobriety; I got my education, and accepted what I called a **higher power** into my life. **Not** God or **Jesus,** just a higher power. What was that power greater than me? I did not know.

This is where I want to remind you and myself that in each situation that turned out correct, I considered myself the hero, never anyone or anything else and certainly not God. This is the misconception that continued to decay the reality and truth of what really was true throughout fifty two years of my life. I had absolutely no understanding of what the words reality or truth really meant or where to find them. I would soon find out and not by my choice because I did not know how.

I never thought that I was hopeless because I always had the material things in life, but I certainly thought life was. Hopeless is one of the words and feelings that showed up often in my life. My immediate response in most of these cases was first **fear,** second anxiety, and third flight, run for my life.

Running away from my life is commonly known as the great geographical cure. There are only two problems with the cure of me running away from what and who I thought was messing up my life. The first delusion in this remedy was the thought that everyone and everything else was the problem. So if I got away from them, my life would change. At times my life would change, but it was always again only a temporary thing.

The second delusion with the running away remedy was that as soon as I got to my unknown destination and felt that I had left all of the problems and mess behind me, sooner rather than later there would be a knock at the door. I would cautiously open the door and guess who was knocking? ME! I was standing on the outside looking in at myself with tons of baggage that I had tried to leave behind me. **I was always stalking myself.** Can you imagine calling any of the authorities on this earth and telling them that I wanted my stalker arrested? Somehow I think I would have been locked up.

My life was all **smoke and mirrors.** I could not run away from myself any longer. The **dysfunction** was now the blood that surged through my empty heart. My problems were no longer the fault of everyone and everything else.

However to my detriment I was still a great **illusionist** and most people looking at my life from the outside in would not have known the agony I was fighting with on a daily basis.

My fifty-two car train was now, filled to the top with my bad actions, broken family, lost friends, addictions, and character defects. Each car was packed and resembled a trash hoarder's home, with the following things that controlled my very being. I had spent my life hoarding these emotions as if they were a valuable collectable, fear, depression, hopelessness, insecurity, selfishness, false pride, low self-esteem, panic and anxiety.

My train full of junk was now barreling down the tracks of life. The speed was at such a pace that the train was only a blur to anyone that it soared by. Due to the lack of my maintaining the engine with the proper tools and guidance, all the working parts of the engine had been pushed to the point of overused stress. But I continued to refuse to believe that anything or anyone other than me was able to be the engineer of my train of life. It was now the time in my life that my lack of knowledge of what really was in the world, and the lack of faith in anything was going to catch up with me.

In one seconds time all went crazy. My train was out of control, skipped the tracks and crashed. The sound effects were deafening from the people involved screaming in anger, others crying from pain. It was all too horrifying and overwhelming for me to face. How had this happened and what could I possibly do to clean up the wreckage? I wanted to do what I had always done in the past and that was to run. But I was forced to turn around and look back. All I could see was a huge pile of wreckage.

This was the day my life as I had known it was laying there in a pile of twisted trash and the sight and realization of this was overwhelming. All the energy and strength in my body to run from this or to continue to deny the mess I had made had been sucked out of me, with the force of the air escaping from a big punctured Good Year Blimp that had been struck by a missile.

I was in critical condition and was rushed to the doors of God's Emergency Room!

IN THE AMBULANCE

*W*hy does life hurt so much?

At this point in my journey I still did not have the answer to that question, but there was an unidentifiable fire burning inside me to find the answer to this lifelong question. I was being guided by an unknown force to find a way to understand what this fire was, and what I could do about it.

Have you ever asked yourself or anyone else why you have had to endure the pains of life here on earth?_____

Has anyone ever asked you this question about their life and you found that you did not have an answer for them? _____

I was being guided by a force other than myself to take a long, hard, demoralizing look at the fact that all I knew and had learned here on earth was worth zero as far as the meaning of true peace in life. My fifty-two car train filled to the very top with my bad actions, broken family, lost friends, addictions and character defects was all the evidence I needed to realize that I needed to search out a new way to exist here on earth. As I inventoried the wreckage of my life I was devastated at what I saw. A great number of these cars where jam packed with garbage that I believed held great value to my life. These cars resembled a trash hoarder's home where the following things had become the controlling factors in my life. They now controlled my very being and the ability for me to not be able to live life. I started to realize that I had spent my life hoarding the following emotions as if they were a valuable commodity, fear, depression, hopelessness, insecurity, selfishness, false pride, low self-esteem, panic and anxiety. They were now the staples of my existence.

GOD'S EMERGENCY WAITING ROOM

I was now sitting in what I now know was God's Emergency Room. I of course was not capable or was not willing to recognize it as this at that time in my life though. There is an old saying "The Walking Dead" and that was me. I wish that I could tell you that this was the day my life changed in ways that could only be explained by a magical cure, but how could that be when I was still the doubting Thomas.

This broken, fatally wounded, human flesh of structure was still not willing to move from the emergency room chair into the triage room for assessment until I could do a lot more research about this new way to heal my heart, soul and body.

Before we get into the definitions of the words underlined in my testimony that I thought were important enough to investigate and see if this was the type of care I really needed. And if this God, Jesus and Bible stuff really did deal with life problems of today, I had to get by my own prejudice and ignorance and stop saying that, "I could not understand the Bible because it had nothing to do with how to live in today's society and that I could not understand the writings any more than Shakespeare's writings years before." I must confess to you that I quite honestly did not have any hope of my research proving me wrong, and I was once and for all, going to give it my all to prove that it did not! Hey, it gave me something to live for and I would do anything to stop living in my own Hell.

So after hard headed consideration and the lack of being able to deal with the pain and confusion, I agreed to go into the Triage room and asses my symptoms.

GOD'S TRIAGE ROOM

*T*he words underlined in my testimony are crucial words in assessing my symptoms. So I needed to understand the relationship between them and the world and them and God. In order for me to prove that God, Jesus and the Bible was not the medicine for me. Or I would have to surrender to the fact that I had wasted a good part of my life being deviant to the only treatment that would heal this broken empty heart.

What came first the Bible or the Dictionary?

Life today is so fast paced and in such turmoil that people like me find it impossible to find a place of peace. Boy, I sure did try though, in many different ways. From hiding in my room, over compensating in everything and everyone, to just giving up and playing with the feel good things that my junk filled mind and heart told me would make me feel better.

Just for identifying purposes let us take a look at the reality shows on television. I am not picking on these programs because I truly think that they have a purpose. They can show us just how many of our countries' citizens are hurting and in most cases they are totally ignorant to their turmoil and how it consumes the peace and joy in life.

I can see myself in many of the people that have agreed to be transparent enough to lay their life out on the tarmac of crucifixion by the world. To those that are saying that these people are doing it for financial gain or fame, maybe some do. Okay, many do! But that is all part of the turmoil hangover. Let us hold back on judgment of them for now, and see what we can learn about them, ourselves and our loved ones.

The following is just a few descriptions of the reality programs that I have watched. I use to watch them for entertainment just like most of the people that watch them, and as you probably know there must be millions of us or these shows would not be on television and multiplying faster than rabbits.

I should have been able to see myself in their image, but let's remember my image was distorted in the mirror.

There are reality shows about hoarders, eating disorders, interventions for drugs and alcohol, young adults partying and sleeping with multiple partners, sweepstakes winners and what they do with the money they always thought they wanted (yah I wanted it to). People with all kinds of obsessive compulsive behaviors, people that come in and help totally dysfunctional parents of young children that have no idea of how to control themselves, families of sports figures and icons that seem to think it is attractive to show that they have nothing to offer their fans as far as moral values.

Last but not least the multiple house wives from whatever state they are from and their nasty family and friendship wars over money, jealousy, jewels, husbands, money, money, money and what about me, me, me.

Please take a strong note in your mind now about the next thing I am going to tell you. I was one of those housewives (not on camera, but I would have if I could have). These shows are rather new to the networks and if you are a follower you should have noticed that life for these women has not stayed as portrayed in the beginning. Some have left the show for their sanity; some have learned that their children are out of control or their marriages are in big trouble because of the show and how it has become their priority. Others have lost their husband's to death, divorce or suicide. A few have lost all the money they had, if they had it at all to begin with.

I must confess my marriage that was in that two percentile money bracket of the country ended and honestly I cannot tell you why. I do not believe that it was lack of love, but my husband and I had signed a legal lease of marriage with a pre-nuptial agreement. He rented me and I was a recipient of what I thought was the amazing, easy lifestyle.

Now here is the shocker, **"none of us are the landlord of anything; everything we have can be repossessed by life in a millisecond. We are ALL lessees.**

"Where is the peace in all this turmoil?"

I would be willing to bet it's not in your head, not in your heart, not in your family, not in your government, not in your finances, and not in your mirror.

The homeless on the street seem to have less turmoil in their life than those of us that think we have it all. But I would guess that somewhere in their life, turmoil brought them to that point. Turmoil unlike people has no prejudice. It loves the poor, the rich, the religious, the healthy or the unhealthy, the good, the bad and the ugly. Do not let it in when it knocks at your door.

Seem impossible? It is not!

Read on with an open heart and the seed of curiosity will be planted in you as it was in me.

The only way that I could be fed and understand the symptoms of my disease was to spoon feed the answers of truth one by one. The following is how I am slowly feeding it to you.

First I have given you the sentence from my testimony that the underlined word to be defined is in.

I have then given you the world's dictionary definition of the word.

The next phase was to try and find a verse in the Bible that relates to the defined word in today's world and finally an explanation of the verse that I could understand and relate to.

Most of the explanations that allow me to learn the truth were read in the well-known and respected: "Thru The Bible" series, written by J. Vernon McGee. This is one of the only recipes of truth that I found soft enough to digest.

I have given them to you after each verse to help you understand the journey that God took me on to get my attention and to let me know that He loves me and He could and would heal me.

ASSCESSING THE SYMPTOMS

My casual friends, acquaintances or any one meeting me for the first time would have had absolutely no idea of the (1) <u>TURMOIL</u> that was castrating my ability to truly enjoy life.

(1) <u>TURMOIL-</u> a state or condition of extreme confusion, agitation or commotion

In verses **Job 3:17-24 (N.I.V.)** before the two I quote bellow Job pictures death as being preferred to life. He says that life is such a burden. He does not want to live. He would rather die. Job says he would welcome death like a miner who is digging for gold and gives a shout of joy when he finds it. He is in a desperate, desolate, condition. Nowhere does it mention him taking his own life, you must know that! He just thinks that he would prefer death to life on this earth.

The words, he does not want to live, he would rather die, I could most assuredly understand. I could not have translated my feeling quite so eloquently, but I sure was able to identify because of the mess my life was at this point. My problem was that I was more afraid of dying than living because I had no idea what death would lead me to, or where, if anything at all. I already knew what life did and did not feel like as horrible or great it might have been.

JOB 3:25-26 (NIV) 25) what I feared has come upon me; what I dreaded has happened to me. 26) I have no peace, no quietness; I have no rest, but only <u>turmoil</u>

Job had been dwelling in peace and prosperity, things were well with him, but the fear of the uncertainty of life was robbing him of his peace. His tranquility even in his days of prosperity was disturbed by the uncertainty of life. I think this is a fear that many people, including me experience. We fear that something terrible is going to happen to us. Job was a faithful man and he still felt the way I feel at times, that impressed me. We do not have to be perfect to be close to God. That certainly contradicted what I had been taught by religion earlier in life.

Something I had to think about: My problem was that I would grab for my earthy security blankets instead of grabbing for the Savior, the only one that can change us!

Lamentations 3:17(NIV) I have been deprived of peace; I have forgotten what prosperity is.

The theme of the book of Lamentations is that God is just, but he is also a God of hope, love, compassion, faithfulness, and salvation, one who does not abandon **those who turn to him** for help. I want to state right here in the beginning, that we are not capable of saving ourselves from turmoil. I and many of you have already tried and found that trying to change yourself just does not work on a long term basis. God is not asking for perfection from you and me he knows that is impossible.

Lamentations 3:22-23 (NIV) 22) Because of the Lord's great love we are not consumed, for his compassions NEVER fail. 23) They are new every morning, great is your faithfulness

I would like you to just take the last year of your life and think of all the choices you have made that would have kept you from even wanting the Lord to look at your life, or for you to look to him for help.

I know the choices made by me are many and in the past I would not have allowed myself to even acknowledge that he existed. Why, because I thought that he would hate me and have shame of me. But most of all I feared his wrath.

The old saying "out of sight out of mind" worked for me.

Or so I thought. Well think about this truth that I have found to be true.

If God did not have mercy, even to those of us that run from him and we really got our just desserts we would have been utterly destroyed by now. We would have disappeared from this earth.

My casual friends, acquaintances or any one meeting me for the first time would have had absolutely no idea of the turmoil that was (2) CASTRATING my ability to truly enjoy life.

(2) CASTRATING – to render **impotent** or **deprive** of vitality especially by psychological means

I needed to look up the word impotent in the context of this definition.

IMPOTENT - Not potent; lacking in power, strength, or vigor: incapable of self-restraint.

I could see after reading these definitions of castrating that I was impotent of enjoyment, not deprived of it, because deprived means to take away or not available. That was not the case in my life. No one except myself deprived me from anything that had to do with enjoying life. The problem was I never knew what true enjoyment was, so how could I enjoy it. I simply had no concept of what it was or how to get it.

John 5:3-6 (NIV) 3) In these lay a multitude of those who were sick, blind, lame, and withered, waiting for the moving of the waters; 4) for an angel of the Lord went down at certain seasons into the pool, and stirred up the water, whoever then first, after the stirring up of the water, stepped in was made well from whatever disease with which he was afflicted. 5) And a certain man was there, who had been thirty-eight years in his sickness. 6) When Jesus saw him lying there, and knew that he had already been a long time in that condition, He said to him, "Do you want to get well?"

Chapter 5 in John brings us to the very essence of healing the impotent. Actually, in a sense, this miracle of healing this invalid is the turning point in the ministry of Jesus Christ. This miracle set the bloodhounds of hate on His track, and they never let up until they put Him to death on the cross.

Do you want to get well? _____

Are you ready to trust that it is a possibility to be well?_____

I must say that at this point in my journey I was not even sure that I ever could get well.

Handly C.G. Moule

I would not have the restless will

That hurries to and fro,

Seeking for some great thing to do

Or secret thing to know;

I would be treated as a child,

And guided where I go.

This poem was very inviting. But was I willing to let go of my control and be treated as a child of God?

My casual friends, acquaintances or any one meeting me for the first time would have had absolutely no idea of the turmoil that was castrating my ability to truly (3) <u>ENJOY</u> life.

(3)   <u>ENJOY</u>- to **take** pleasure or satisfaction in

To take pleasure or satisfaction, how interesting! **Take:** that is a word that was a front seat passenger on my train of life. I would never have admitted it in a million years, but it was one of the biggest revelations I was going to have in the near future.

Have you ever thought of how many times you have just taken your pleasure, no matter what the cost was to you or others?_____

You may be like me and if honest you have to answer that with a strong yes. I had no idea how many times I acted out of the desire for pleasure without even giving it a thought.

Some may say that what I am stating here is just semantics. Do not fool yourself I have found that when I use the word semantics I am in most cases, looking for a reason to excuse something I want or something I want to do when I know it is wrong. In these cases I am just rationalizing my right to do what is wrong. If your pleasure is found in things you know are not correct, you are taking that pleasure or better yet stealing it.

I promise you that your enjoyment is only a synthetic sugar and your satisfaction from that false sugar high is not real and it will not last. It will be SWEET but LOW! And it will never be EQUAL to the gift of true enjoyment and knowing the truth of what true pleasure is.

In the following verse you will see that God wants you to have it all, but it is a sad story when we do not realize that it is him that gives it to us. Do not be as stubborn as I was and let strangers **enjoy** the gifts God means for you through Jesus.

ECCLESIASTES 6:1-2 I have seen another evil under the sun, and it weighs heavily on men. God gives a man wealth, possessions and honor, so that he lacks nothing his heart desires, but God does not enable him to enjoy them, and a stranger <u>enjoys</u> them instead. This is meaningless grievous evil.

Solomon is the writer of this book. This book is the dramatic autobiography of Solomon's life when he was away from God. Man has tried to be happy without God; it is being tried by millions of people in today's world also. I was one of those lost souls; the book of Ecclesiastes shows the absurdity of the attempt to understand enjoyment without the understanding it is a gift that comes with faith.

Solomon was the wisest of men, and he had a wisdom that was God-given. He tried every field of endeavor and pleasure that was known to man and his conclusion was that all is vanity. The word vanity means "empty, purposeless". Satisfaction and enjoyment in life can never be attained in this manner.

My casual friends, acquaintances or any one meeting me for the first time would have had absolutely no idea of the turmoil that was castrating my ability to truly enjoy <u>LIFE.</u>

(4)   <u>**LIFE**</u> The spiritual existence transcending physical death. A specific phase of earthly existence from life to death

JOHN 5:12 whoever has the Son has life: whoever does not have the Son of God docs not have life.

This verse alone with no simple translation is very scary for those of us that do not believe in God or Jesus. Do not overlook the translation below it is very eye opening.

"He that hath the Son hath life. John did not say, he that belongs to a church has life." There are those that say "I am a Baptist", "I am a Methodist", "I am a Presbyterian" or "I am a Nazarene" or I belong to the Church of God." It does not matter what church you belong to nor does church membership mean you are saved.

Then what does it mean to be saved?

"He that hath the Son hath life." The questions are, do you have Christ? Is he your savior? Do you trust him in such a way that nothing on this earth or in heaven can shake your confidence in him?

Allow me to consider you my friend, because when I share the most intimate facts of my life with someone I consider them a friend. In that since you may not know me in my flesh, but you will now know me better than many that have seen me in the flesh a multitude of times, including most of those that have had intimate relationships with me.

Why, because through the Lord I am able to be transparent and because of that we are sharing the word of God. I also hope that we become brothers and sisters within the Lord's family.

Do not feel you are different if you do not trust enough to open your heart, ears, mind and soul yet. But be proud that you are opening your eyes.

Yes, you are opening your eyes, or He has opened them for you because without your eyes being open you could not read this.

WAS I LOST?

"What circumstances in my life would leave me in such <u>despair?</u>"

<u>DESPAIR</u>- to lose or **abandon** hope: be or become hopeless

When I first looked at this definition the only word I was drawn to was the word hopeless. But upon further investigation the word **abandon** stuck in my head. So I had to do further investigation. Abandon means to walk away from.

Was my despair my choice?

Had I walked away from hope?

Or did I even know what the word hope meant?

2Corinthians 4: 3(NIV) But if our gospel be hid, it is to them that are <u>lost</u>:

Oh wow! To them that are lost: Would you say that I was lost in life at this time? I had to have known that I was, because of the pain and despair that I was experiencing inside of me. But I do not think that I was ready to totally admit that I was the one that was lost, yet. I was also still more comfortable blaming God for the defects in me and my life, than I was willing to believe that he loved me and wanted to heal my sinning heart.

2Corinthians 4:4(NIV) in whom the God of <u>this world</u> hath <u>blinded the minds of them which believe not</u>, lest the light of the glorious gospel of Christ, who is the image of God, should shine unto them

Some feel that "God of this world" should be translated to "God of this Age" the truth is that it is still and always will be God's world. He is the creator, but sin has married this age.

Satan is the God of this age and we are allowing him to run it. Satan has "blinded the minds of them which will believe not." I am not the only one in this age that says things like the following.

"I do not understand the gospel (Bible)."

"I have heard of it my whole life, but it does not mean anything to me or today's life."

Why do we feel and believe this? Because the devil has blinded our eyes so we cannot see.

God is the source of our light but he never takes away our choice to stay in the dark. Despair is one of the feelings of darkness!

Have you reached for the light switch on your wall lately to take away the darkness in a room? I have, and I do not question the fact that when I reach for that switch the light will come on and guide my way, as long as I have paid the electric bill.

Paid the bill, may sound as if I am making a poor effort at being funny, but I realized that I always thought that I could never pay the bill of the Lord. I never knew that Jesus had already paid the bill to take me out of the darkness.

How do you pay the bill to God? By believing in his Son Jesus and having faith in why he sent him to die for us. The faith that Jesus was sent to die for our sins will be the start of lighting up your whole life rather than the light bulb connected to that switch on the wall that will only light up that room.

I held only two positions in the circumstances that showed themselves in my life. The first being that I was always the <u>victim</u>.

<u>Victim</u>– one who is killed, injured or subjected to **<u>suffering.</u>**

One that is killed is most certainly a victim to whatever circumstance killed him. One that is injured by another was a victim at that moment of injury. But just how long do we stay a victim to that evil deed?

I however was the type of person that was always addicted to suffering. I also was the originating cause or motive of my suffering in many cases. My suffering usually originated with my own bad choices and also followed my own agenda.

I could not remove myself from the feeling of suffering and I took it like a drug. It made me feel alive. Poor me, Poor me! I had a ring around my bottom from sitting on the pity pot.

Now I am not going to try to fool you into believing that there is not going to be suffering in your life from the moment you start having a relationship with Jesus. But instead of suffering being your main course at the table of life it will be your side dish. The table will also be set with the correct utensils, so you will be able to eat and digest the suffering in a palatable way.

Imagine how good that Filet Mignon would taste, if you were used to eating mud pies.

PSALM 10: 13-14 (NIV) why does the wicked man revile God? Why does he say to himself, "He won't call me to account"? 14) But you, O God, do see trouble and grief; you are the helper of the fatherless.

Not only did I not believe in God, but I despised Him. It is inconsistent to despise someone who does not exist; obviously He has to be, for someone to store up this kind of bitterness and hatred. When he says "He won't call me to account," he is saying that there is no judgment."

In today's culture there are a great number of people saying there is no God, or if there is, He is too far away for them to bother with; and they are confident there will be no judgment. Well if we continue to take this position than anything goes in this world. God may be the most unpopular person in the world right now. Why? It is simple because the evil are controlling the train. We have moved toward the time when the "sin of man" has become "man of sin," this will be the final Antichrist.

Turn your enemies over to God.

Turn over those who would betray you to the Lord, **including yourself**. I was astounded in the fact that the Lord wanted me to turn even my own betrayals of myself to him. Do any of us realize how many times we betray ourselves in a given day? It could be as small as not brushing our teeth in the morning (that is also a betrayal to those around us), or as large as pretending that our heart is not broken when it is and not dealing with healing it.

Denial by you of anything going on in your life or how you are affecting others' lives is a form of betrayal to all. I have found that God does a much better job than I could ever do in dealing with my enemies and my demons and he is more than happy to do so. **In his way, at his time and at his will!**

Romans 12:19 do not take revenge, my friends, but leave room for God's wrath, for it is written: "It is mine to avenge; I will repay, "says the Lord.

Most of us find it hard not to strike back when we feel we have been wronged in any way. I was better at defense maneuvers than most sports team defensive members could ever be. If you looked at me in what I thought was the wrong way (grilled me) I would immediately set myself up with the famous, you dare to look at me that way, you judgmental, low life, ugly person, I am better than you. This look was not at all a pretty look, but most of us have one.

The sad part of this scenario is that I have found that in most cases these people were not even noticing me, never mind grilling me, unless of course I was causing a scene for some other reason, such as yelling at a cashier that was not working as fast as I thought they should. Why, are we always on the defensive ready to strike out?

Once we take any of these matters into our own hands and attempt to work these things out by hitting back as hard as we can, we have taken the matter and the consequences out of God's control.

I also would have sworn that I was victimized by <u>God</u>!

GOD- (capitalized) Noun- the ONE Supreme Being and ruler of the universe

1 Thessalonians 2:13- **And we also thank God continually because, when you received the word of God, which you heard from us, you accepted it not as a human word, but as it actually is, the word of God, which is indeed at work in you who believe.**

How do you receive the Word of God? Do you receive it as the Word of God, or do you get angry and scared like I did.

Does the hair stand up on the back of your neck when someone approaches you with their Christian faith, Jesus and the Bible? When it did for me it was because I was taking the word of God personal to my sins. I believed that I was being judged by those that were trying to give it to me. But in all cases I was the one doing the judging. I was judging them and the word of God.

God's word can be like salt to some of us. It stings when it gets into a fresh wound of sin in the life of an individual. God's word is also the light, but some of us make the decision to stay in the darkness of evil. Because we are afraid and feel that we cannot comprehend what is expected of us.

Friends please just take God's word as the fact that God is trying to communicate with you and if the first person to deliver his word is someone you feel you cannot identify with, then ask God for someone that you can understand. God will answer your request and God will never take away your freedom to make your own choices!

WHERE DO WE FIND THE WORD OF GOD? IN THE BIBLE!

<u>god</u> (not capitalized) Any person or thing made chief object of ones love, inspiration or aspiration: Money is his/her *god*.

I was inquisitive when I looked up the definition of God in the dictionary and found that it was listed both with a capital G and a lower case g. There is only one God but we here on earth worship many other gods. At first site I thought that this definition meant that we were not to worship another God or idol under any other name and it does mean that. But there is also much more meaning to this definition. We are not to put other things that we desire, want and need before God. God wants you to have all your needs met and he will make that happen in his will, when you have the Holy Spirit in your heart. Nothing should come before your love for God.

Deuteronomy 5: 7 (NIV) Thou shalt have no other <u>gods</u> before me

Man's first sin was not to become or be an atheist, it was to become a polytheist. Polytheist is the worship of many gods such as statues, saints, money and power. There is only one God!

On occasion when the good feelings of <u>pleasure</u> or happiness, showed themselves in my life, did I give God the credit?

    (1) PLEASURE to gratify: **GRATIFY-** reward, satisfy, indulge

Proverbs 10:2 3 **a fool finds <u>pleasure</u> in wicked schemes, but a person of understanding delights in wisdom**

Wow, hold on one minute here, wisdom? That is a word that I never put much thought into. Sure I have been called a "wise guy" many times in life, but just what is wisdom? I knew what intelligence meant but wisdom was an unknown. I had to find out just what this word had to do with anything!

WISDOM- knowledge, insight, judgment

The word wisdom in scripture means "the ability to use knowledge aright." The word wisdom is used thirty seven times in the book of Proverbs alone. It is a very important word in the Bible. I have been one of those people in life that have a great deal of knowledge; yet I definitely lacked the wisdom of how to use that knowledge in most of my daily affairs.

2 Chronicles 1: 10-12 10) (NIV) Give me wisdom and knowledge, that I may lead this people, for who is able to govern this great people of yours? 11) God said to Solomon, "Since this is your heart's desire and you have not asked for a long life but for wisdom and knowledge to govern my people whom I have made you king, 12) therefore wisdom and knowledge will be given to you. And I will also give you wealth, riches and honor, such as no king who was before you ever had and none after you will have.

Solomon was granted the wisdom to oversee the empire, but if you read on you will find out that he did not have that same wisdom in spiritual discernment of his own personal life.

    God wants us to have pleasure in life! But if you pick pleasure without using wisdom you will pay the consequences of that choice through life itself. Not having wisdom is not abnormal when one does not have the Holy Spirit in their heart. The book of Proverbs taught me how to start receiving the grace of God's wisdom.

<u>Daniel 4:2-3 </u>**(NIV) 2) it is my <u>pleasure</u> to tell you about the miraculous signs and wonders that the Most High God has performed for me. 3) How great are his signs, how mighty his**

wonders! His kingdom is an eternal kingdom; his dominion endures from generation to generation.

When I share these verses with you I most assuredly can speak from the heart and in truth. I cannot find words divine enough to explain the pleasure I feel as I work on these writings. I am gifted with a very unfamiliar pleasure and peace in my heart; I am honestly comfortable within my human flesh. In future writings of God's Emergency Room I will share some of the wonders and miracles that The Most High God has performed within me and for me.

Proverbs 18:2 Fools find no <u>pleasure</u> in understanding but delight in airing their own opinions.

"If you stop and think before you speak, you will not have to worry afterward about what you said before." Have you ever delivered your opinion all wrapped up looking like the Encyclopedia of knowledge to someone when you knew that the advice in it was one with no true knowledge. But you loved to hear yourself talk. I would often do this knowing now that my opinions were not those of knowledge only ego.

Do not let other peoples' opinion scare you, and do not scare others with yours!

On occasion when the good feelings of pleasure or <u>happiness</u>, showed themselves in my life, did I give God the credit?

   (2)   **HAPPINESS**- a state of wellbeing and contentment: Joy

Ecclesiastes 2:26 (NIV) To the person who pleases him, God gives wisdom, knowledge and <u>happiness</u>, but to the sinner he gives the task of gathering and storing up wealth to hand it over to the one who pleases God. This too is meaningless, a chasing after the wind.

If you are living just for self, whether you are God's child or a degenerated sinner, it will lead to nothing. It will lead to bitterness in your heart, and you will be holding nothing but dead leaves in your hands at the end.

I was inflicted with the false thought that I was always the <u>hero</u> and the one that hit it out of the park each time with no help from anyone or anything least of all God.

<u>**HERO-**</u> a person distinguished for exceptional **<u>courage</u>**, fortitude, or bold enterprise especially in times of war.

As I read this definition I was embarrassed at the audacity I had in thinking that I was the hero of anything I had ever done. How could I compare myself and the doings to those men and women that have truly had exceptional courage? I was afraid of the whole world, and have never had the fortitude to follow through on anything that had any meaning to anyone but me, and at times that was doubtful also. I could not even save myself from myself. The thought also came to me that when I watched a hero being awarded for their courage, in most cases they honored God for the strength to achieve what they had done.

What is that all about?

Deuteronomy 31:8 the Lord himself goes before you and will be with you; he will never leave you nor forsake you. Do not be afraid: do not be discouraged.

That says it all to the question above. What is that all about?

I want to give you some examples of my <u>ignorance</u> to the truths about this life on earth, and how that lack of knowledge made me feel the way I did in the statements above.

(1) **IGNORANCE**- lack of knowledge, education or awareness

1Timothy 1:13-16 (NIV) 13) even though I was once a blasphemer and a persecutor and a violent man, I was shown mercy because I acted in <u>ignorance</u> and unbelief. 14) The grace of our Lord was poured out on me abundantly, along the faith and love that are in Christ Jesus. 15) Here is a trustworthy saying that deserves acceptance: Christ Jesus came into the world to save sinners- of whom I am the worst. 16) But for that very reason I was shown mercy so that in me, the worst of sinners, Christ Jesus might display his unlimited patients as an example for those who would believe on him and receive eternal life.

Here Paul uses the word blasphemer to describe himself in the past, he hated the Lord Jesus. Yet when Paul speaks of his salvation he says he was saved by the grace of God. It was the mercy of God that put him into ministry. These are the things that will be manifested in the life of a believer. Verse fifteen is an important verse of scripture because it affirms that "Christ Jesus came into the world to SAVE the sinners." He did not come to be the greatest teacher that the world has ever known, although he was. He did not come to set a moral example, but he did that. He came into the world to save sinners. Jesus is the ONLY one that could save me and he is the ONLY one that can save you. And he does it with open arms and love.

You may have been **ignorant** up to now, but now that the seed has been planted in your head about God's grace and mercy, you cannot pretend to be ignorant to the truth anymore. You may choose to ignore it but it is there to stay. God will continue trying to connect with you and show you the way out of the pain with the true diagnoses.

It is exactly as if you went to the hospital emergency room and you were given a prescription to go get some test to diagnose your pain, but you decide not to do as suggested for whatever reason. The fact that you have no knowledge of what is causing the pain will haunt you even if the pain subsides for a period of time.

I want to give you some examples of my ignorance to the <u>truths</u> about this life on earth, and how that lack of knowledge made me feel the way I did in the statements above.

(2) **TRUTHS-** *a* the state of being the case: the body of real things, events, and facts **:a transcendent fundamental or spiritual reality**

Hebrews 5:12 in fact, though by this time you ought to be teachers, you need someone to teach you the elementary <u>truths</u> of God's word all over again. You need milk, not solid food!

This verse relates to Christians that should be matured in their walk with the Lord, but are not. They may not have ever matured or have back slid in the <u>Word</u> so they act like a child that needs to be spoon fed about things such as gossiping, judgment, forgiveness and truth.

For those of us like me that do not understand the word or do not want to understand how it relates to us and our life, we also need to be spoon fed. Think of it like a baby, they cannot chew solid food because they have no teeth to break down the food to a size capable of swallowing. I did not have the teeth of faith so I could not have swallowed all this information without chocking on it. This is why I am trying to pass on the Lord's words in a translation that we may comprehend no matter who we are or where we are in our life here on earth.

Jesus automatically knew what the people in his day needed to hear and how to deliver it straight to their hearts where it needs to be. I believe he tells us how to relate his hope to others that are faith challenged according to today's needs.

Do we listen?

Do not misunderstand me, the Lords word in the Bible will never change and God's word is the only way to be able to handle life on life's terms. However all minds do not learn at the same pace and are not capable of understanding things in the same manner. Some people's minds like to fool them into thinking we understand when we really don't. Do not be afraid of the truth. It took me time to acquire the taste for it and it is now my favorite meal.

I want to give you some examples of my ignorance to the truths about this life on earth, and how that lack of <u>knowledge</u> made me feel the way I did in the statements above.

(3)   **Knowledge;** the fact or conditions of knowing something with familiarity gain through **experience or association**, the **range** of one's information or understanding, the **fact** or condition of having information or of being **learned**

Colossians 2:3 in whom are hidden all the treasures of wisdom and knowledge

The following short saying that I read in J. Vernon McGee stirred up my curiosity to find a way to understand anything that had to do with God or Jesus.

"Next to knowing, is knowing where to find out."

You are right at this moment at the entrance to your destination!

I do this in hope of helping you in understanding how a <u>heart</u> empty of faith and The Holy Spirit , cannot experience, feel or understand, anything with clarity and honest thoughts.

(1)   **HEART-** the emotional or moral as distinguished from the intellectual nature: one's innermost character, feelings, or inclinations: the central or innermost part the essential or most vital part of something

My heart was weak from the lack of healthy emotional and moral exercise (the act of bringing into play or realizing in action). My character had become a cartoon that some would laugh at but others including myself would cry for it. My feelings were negative, angry and raw or they were dead with numbness. The last part of this definition is an awakening for me: the central or innermost part the essential or most vital part of something. My heart the most vital part of me was empty and hardened to stone.

Ezekiel 36:25-26 25) I will sprinkle clean water on you, and you will be clean, I will cleanse you from all your impurities and from all your idols. 26] I will give you a new heart and put a new spirit in you; I will remove from you your heart of stone and give you a heart of flesh.

Where does it say that you are capable of changing your stony heart? It does not! God says what He is going to do. A change is going to take place. "A new heart also I will give you "-----They will be born again.

Psalm 73:26 my flesh and my heart may fail, but God is the strength of my heart and my portion forever.

God knows that we will fail both in our strength and in our heart, but we need to surrender to the fact that He is the strength of our heart. Friend, just trust in this, I have found through the action of the Lord that this is truth. How amazing it is that I was gifted a new life. We always say in life, "If I only knew then what I know now." Well here is your chance. Imagine being born again knowing what you have already experience without the strength of God and having the choice to learn new things with him.

Ecclesiastes 2:10 (NIV) I denied myself nothing my eyes desired; I refused my heart no pleasure. My heart took delight in all my labor, and this was the reward for all my toil.

Imagine walking through this world being able to afford and do all things that your heart desires. You would think that all in that position would be happy. Well most are not. It is said that there are more suicides and deaths due to reckless behavior in the wealthy communities than there are in the homeless and the people that are down and out. I refused my heart no pleasure" Pleasure cannot hold in a heart that is broken or full of holes. It will just flow through

Hebrews 1: 1- 1) faith is being sure of what we hope for <u>and certain of what we do not see</u>. 2) This is what the ancients were commended for. 3) By faith we understand that the universe was formed at God's command, so that what is seen was not made up of what was visible.

I do this in hope of helping you in understanding how a heart empty of <u>faith</u> and The Holy Spirit , cannot experience, feel or understand, anything with clarity and honest thoughts.

(2) **FAITH** – Belief without need of certain proof, Belief in God or in testimony about God as recorded in scriptures

There are certain beliefs that the book of Hebrews rest on. The same as when you study geometry, there are certain axioms with which you must begin, and if you do not, you cannot begin at all. If one plus one does not equal two, then you are out to lunch as far as mathematics is concerned. Also it has been proven that a straight line is the shortest distance between two points and this is accepted. When a fact is established, you can move on and prove something else.

The Bible makes no effort to try to prove God's existence. Look at it as you do any other history event. When you read any writings of history you have faith that it is true even though you were not there.

How can we walk outside and look at all the beauty and miracles and say that there is no creator? "Certain of what we do not see" but we do see the world around us. In realizing that, I was able to start looking into what I could not see and have faith that it really did exist!

Certain proof, where in my life had I found certain proof of anything other than, when left to my own devices I would in most cases fall short of my and other peoples' expectations? Even the proof of that was not a certainty, because there were times in my life when I met the mark that I had aimed for.

Do we ever really have certain proof of anything? I have come to believe no, except for the one huge certainty that we all must face and that is that ALL of us will experience death of the flesh.

In the past I refused to even look into having faith in God. One of my excuses was that no one could prove it to me. Let's face it I just did not want to believe in Him or His Son.

How can I say that?

Do we have proof that when we are ill and the doctor prescribes us a medicine to take that it will work?

NO!

We do not even know that it will not harm us more. But we have to have faith to take the medication. Do we have proof that the food we purchase from a store is going to be safe for us to eat and have the ingredients it says it has to sustain us? No! But we put faith in the humans that are growing, processing and packaging it.

Do we not try to have faith in everything we do on a daily basis?

Well, I decided that I had to have faith and try it just like everyone else that believes did, before God would be able to reveal the certain proof of faith in Him to my heart.

At the beginning I thought that I had to find the faith that I did not have. That is not the case I just had to want to believe and open my heart to God. If I had only known that my rebellion of God was leaving me out there alone. That is why I could not see my way out of the darkness. I always needed proof and all that I could prove is that I was a mess.

Romans 10:9-11 that if you confess with your mouth, "Jesus is Lord," and believe in your heart that God raised Him from the dead, you will be saved. For it is with your heart that you believe and are justified, and it is with your mouth that you confess and are saved. As the scripture says, "Anyone who trusts Him will never be put to shame."

There are many people that maintain that a believer has to make a public confession of faith. That is not what Paul is saying here. Just because you go forward in a public meeting or church does not mean that you have been saved. Paul is saying that we need to bring into agreement our confession and our life. The mouth and the heart should be in harmony, saying the same thing. It is with your heart that you believe. Your "heart" means your total personality, your entire being. You see there are some people who say something with their mouths, they call this lip service to God, but their hearts are far from him. This was me at the beginning, I don't think I did it intentionally I just did not understand it yet. But I was WILLING to try. If there is confession without faith, it is due either to self-deception or to hypocrisy. If there is faith without confession, it may be cowardice.

I do this in hope of helping you in understanding how a heart empty of faith and 3) The Holy Spirit , cannot experience, feel or understand, anything with clarity and honest thoughts.

(3)   HOLY SPIRIT

<u>Holy</u>- Regarded with reverence because associated with or derived from God;

<u>Spirit</u>- The vital essence or animating force in living organisms, especially man, often considered **divine** in origin.

The doctrine of the Trinity- God the Father, God the Son and God the **Holy Spirit** are each equally and eternally the ONE true God-this is admittedly difficult to comprehend, and yet it is the very foundation of Christian truth.

John 14: 8-26 (NIV) 8) Philip said, "Lord, show us the father and that will be enough for us." 9) Jesus answered: "Don't you know me, Philip even after I have been among you such a long time? Anyone who has seen me has seen the Father. How can you say, "Show us the Father?" 10) Don't you believe that I am in the Father, and that the Father is in me? The words I say to you are not just my own. Rather, it is the Father, living in me, who is doing his work. 11) Believe me when I say that I am in the Father and the Father is in me; or at least believe on the evidence of the miracles themselves. 12) I tell you the truth, anyone who has faith in me will do what I have been doing. He will do even greater things than these, because I am going to the Father. 13) And I will do whatever he asked in my name, so that the Son may bring glory to the Father. 14) You may ask me for anything in my name, and I will do it.

<u>Jesus Promises the HOLY SPIRIT</u>

15) If you love me, you will obey what I command. 16) And I will ask the Father, and he will give you another <u>Counselor</u> to be with you forever- 17) the spirit of the truth. The world cannot accept him, because it neither sees him nor knows him. But you know him, for he lives with you and will be in you. 18) I will never leave in you as orphans; I will come to you. 19)

Before long, the world will not see me anymore but you will see me. Because I live, you will also live. 20) On that day you will realize that I am in my father, and you are in me, and I am in you. 21) Whoever has my commands and obeys them, he is the one who loves me. He who loves me will be loved by my father, and I too will love him and show myself to him." 22) Then Judas (not Judas Iscariot) said, "But Lord, why do you intend to show yourself to us and not to the world?" 23) Jesus replied, "If anyone loves me, he will obey my teaching. My Father will love him, and we will come to him and make our home with him. 24) He who does not love me will not obey my teaching. These words you hear are not my own; they belong to my Father who sent me. 25) "All this I have spoken while still with you. 26) But the Counselor, the Holy Spirit, whom the Father will send in my name, will teach you all things and will remind you of everything I have said to you.

John16:12-14 (NIV) 12) "I have much more to say to you, more than you can bear.13) But when he the spirit of truth, comes, he will guide you into the truth. 14) He will not speak on his own; he will speak only what he hears and he will tell you what is yet to come. He will bring glory to me by taking what is mine and making it known to you.

I do not know it all. We are to keep growing in grace and in knowledge of Him.

How can we do that?

Just reading the Bible is not the complete answer; the **Holy Spirit** must be our teacher as we read. The Spirit of God is the spirit of Truth. He will lead and guide you into the truth. The snag here is that you have to willing for the guidance.

I do this in hope of helping you in understanding how a heart empty of faith and The Holy Spirit cannot experience, feel or understand, anything with clarity and <u>honest</u> thoughts.

(4)   **HONEST-** Free from fraud or deception: legitimate, truthful, genuine, real, humble, reputable, respectable, good, worthy, creditable, praiseworthy, frank, and innocent.

Proverbs 12: 17-22 17) A truthful witness gives honest testimony, but a false witness tells lies. 18) Reckless words pierce like a sword, but the tongue of the wise brings healing. 19) Truthful lips endure forever, but a lying tongue last only a moment. 20) There is deceit in the hearts of those who plot evil, but joy for those who promote peace. 21) No harm befalls the righteous but the wicked have their fill of trouble. 22) The Lord detests lying lips, but delights in men who are truthful.

In verse 17 it talks about giving honest testimony. Your life is your testimony including all your mistakes and sins. All testimonies told in the Bible are transparent and honest, some so honest that it is hard to believe that God still loved the sinner in them and used his love to heal the sinner. My friend, if these testimonies were not told in honesty how could the word and promises of God be True? Your testimony is only of value to God if told in total honesty.

An honest Pastor that takes the risk of preaching the truth is without a doubt at times going to put a sword through your heart. And if you are not honest to and about yourself you will take on the emotions of hatred and bitterness toward that pastor.

In verse 19-21 all that is being told here is concerning the tongue, the lying tongue and the lips of truth. The Word of God has more to say about the tongue, more judgment on the abuse of the tongue, than it is has to say about the use and abuse of alcohol. Yet it is interesting that a lying tongue and a gossip can get by in some Christian circles today, whereas a drunkard may be more easily rejected by us.

In verse 22 it is stated that a very important characteristic of a child of God is his truthfulness.

I pray that those of you that are reading my testimony will learn that the most important <u>factor</u> for this equation is that I be very transparent with you about all of my character defects, rebellion, confusion and the huge mistakes that I have made.

(1) FACTOR- one that actively contributes to the production of a result

Do you realize how much you, your actions and faith or lack of it contributes to the results of what your future will bring?

In life we contribute to the production of many results, some good, some bad, but just how much do I want to contribute to what God wants for my life?

1 Peter 4: 2 As a result, they do not live the rest of their earthly lives for evil human desires, but rather for the will of God.

To be spiritually minded is true life and peace. The only way for us to have that life and peace is to be in a close fellowship with Jesus. If we say that we are in fellowship with him and continue to walk in darkness, we lie and do not live in truth.

What keeps you from being the factor that gives you the life of light?_____
_____

I pray that those of you that are reading my testimony will learn that the most important factor for this <u>equation</u> is that I be very transparent with you about all of my character defects, rebellion, confusion and the huge mistakes that I have made.

(2)   **EQUATION-an element affecting a <u>process</u>: a state of close association or identification**

Life is an equation with many unknown factors and there is a process to solving each equation. However the second part of the definition tells us a close association or identification let's take a look at those words.

Romans 8:15-16 for you did not receive a spirit that makes you a slave again to fear, but you received the Spirit of <u>son ship</u>. And by him we cry, Abba, Father. The Spirit himself testifies with our spirit that we are God's children.

The X factor in my equation was to have a close association with and identify myself through God. He is my father and he knows all of my unanswered questions and holds the answers to them also.

The unknown factors may never be revealed to you because they are only known by the Lord. Therefore it is imperative that you have a close association with the Lord for him to reveal the unknown factors at his will.

I pray that those of you that are reading my testimony will learn that the most important factor for this equation is that I be very <u>transparent</u> with you about all of my character defects, rebellion, confusion and the huge mistakes that I have made.

(3)   **TRANSPARENT- free from pretense or deceit: characterized by visibility or accessibility of information about oneself.**

Revelation 21:21 (NIV) the twelve gates were twelve pearls, each gate made of a single pearl. The great street of the city was of pure gold, like transparent glass.

The definition of transparent above sounds humanly impossible when you give it great thought and it is. Free from pretense or deceit, I really was never free from pretense or deceit but I would give the **pretense** that I was.

There was a very famous statement that freely shot out of my mouth that went like this, "I don't care what people think of me or what I am doing."

How far into denial can one get?

Of course I cared what people thought of me, or I would not have had the need the say those words to another in that context. Of course we care what people think about us and our situations, or we would not pretend we are of sound mind, emotions and heart when we are in trouble or hurting so bad that we want to escape from reality.

To be visible and accessible of information about yourself is something I highly suggest that you do only under the control and watch of the Lord. The world can be mean and people's tongues can be deadly to those that are not wearing the God's suit of armor. When you service the Lord by sharing your honest testimony with those that could be helped by it, it is only through God's strength and grace that you will survive the evil tongues of the sick and fearful.

Ephesians 6:11 (NIV) Put on the full armor of God, so that you can take your stand against the devil's schemes.

You cannot overcome the Devil in your strength and your own power. "Be strengthened by the Lord"- that is the ONLY place you and I can get power.

<u>I pray that the Lord keeps my testimony and life like transparent glass!</u>

I pray that those of you that are reading my testimony will learn that the most important factor for this equation is that I be very transparent with you about all of my character defects, <u>rebellion</u>, confusion and the huge mistakes that I have made.

(4)   **REBELLION- opposition to one in authority or dominance; open armed and usually unsuccessful defiance of or resistance.**

ISAIAH 65:2 (NIV) All day long I have held out my hands to an obstinate people, who walk in ways not good, pursuing their own imagination.

This verse is from the Old Testament of the Bible and was at the time directed to the Jewish population in the nation of Israel. The gospel was given to the Jew first. This verse is very important to all people today. It is clear that what is being stated here in today's lingo is that once you have heard the truth of God and refuse to open your heart to the truth, you are left to your own devices and life's obstacles.

So if I rejected the word he would move on to those that will not. MY LOSS! Thank you God for not giving up on me!

You are at this point reading my testimony and it is full of the truth of God, therefore if you refuse to open your heart and mind you will be left to your devices. I will be praying for those of you that are still addicted to the world of rebellion.

I pray that those of you that are reading my testimony will learn that the most important factor for this equation is that I be very transparent with you about all of my character defects, rebellion, confusion and the huge <u>mistakes</u> that I have made.

(5)   **MISTAKES**- to **blunder** in **choices** to move unsteadily or confusedly

Plunder: To make a mistake through stupidity, ignorance, or carelessness

Well I believe that it is time to revisit the word, choices yet again.

Oh wisdom! To have you and be able to make the correct choices, where are you?

PROVERBS 8: 1-12 1) Does not wisdom call out? Does not understanding raise her voice? 2) On the heights alone the way, where the paths meet, she takes her stand; 3) beside the gates leading into the city, at the entrances, she cries aloud: 4)To you, O men, I call out; I raise my voice to all mankind. 5) You who are simple gain prudence, you who are foolish, gain understanding. 6) Listen, for I have worthy things to say; I open my lips to speak what is right. 7) My mouth speaks what is right. 7) My mouth speak what is true, for my lips detest wickedness. 8) All the words of my mouth are just; none of them are crooked or perverse. 9) To the discerning all of them are right; they are faultless to those who have knowledge. 10) <u>Choose</u> my instruction instead of silver, knowledge rather than choice gold, 11) for wisdom is more precious than rubies, and nothing you desire can compare to her. 12) I wisdom, dwell together with prudence; I possess knowledge and discretion.

I love Proverbs; Proverbs are sayings that convey a specific truth in a pointed pithy way. Proverbs are short sentences drawn from long experience and are couched in a form that is easy to remember and philosophy based on experience and a rule of conduct.

Solomon is the writer of Proverbs and it has been said that there are some characteristics and features of the Book of Proverbs that should be noted.

(1)   Proverbs bears no unscientific statement or inaccurate observation.

(2)   Proverbs is a book of a high moral plane.

(3)   The Proverbs do not contradict themselves, while man's proverbs may often.

Some have said that there is nothing about the gospel in proverbs. I have learned through those that have gone before me that this is not the truth. The one in this book whose wisdom it is, is none other than the Lord Jesus Christ!

Here is something that you can take to the bank, "if anything is real wisdom, it is simple and it will appeal to the simple." I find it amazing how some people think certain things are so profound and when you examine it, it is not at all. It is just wisdom and simplicity. I used to think simplicity was a swear word.

Ladies, throughout the verses quoted above it refers to wisdom as "she" that peaked my curiosity. Had I been correct my whole life when I would state that men were not equipped with that great character trait, because it was a she? It is a great stab to my ego that I tell you I was wrong on more than one account.

The first being that the word "she" is used when referring to wisdom because it is a noun famine in Hebrew, therefore when translated to human form it is a she. I offer my sincere apologies' to men for my past anger and ignorance.

My second misconception in life about wisdom is that I had or have it. I did not, and it is through the research for these writings that I have been gifted the revelation that I no longer have to be clueless and continue to make huge mistakes.

I know through my faith in Jesus that if I search out wisdom in the word I will be graced with God's wisdom and receive His gift for me to be able to make the correct choices. This will not happen without me searching for the truth in his word, nor does it mean I will not make mistakes while I learn. But I take great comfort knowing that God allows me to succeed through my failures if I trust him to teach me.

I know that is not an easy thing to do and you may be <u>scared</u>, I know I was.

SCARED- thrown into or being in a state of fear, fright or panic

1 John 4:18 (NIV) There is no fear in love. But perfect love drives out fear, because fear has to do with punishment. The one who fears is not made perfect in love

There is nothing worse than fear in the human heart. Ask me I know firsthand! But the child of God does not need to fear any judgment. It was all settled when Christ died on the cross. If you are fearful, than you cannot enjoy your life and or your salvation, peace and Joy stems from love, and if you have love for the Lord Jesus, for God and The Holy Spirit lives within you, then fear has been cast out.

There are no <u>secrets</u> between you and God whether you believe that or not.

SECRETS – something hidden or unexplained

Proverbs 15:11 (The Message) Even hell holds no secrets from God— do you think he can't read human heads.

God is the discerner of the thoughts and intents of the heart. He knows what we are doing and not doing. Only God can reveal what is on the other side in the unseen world. So do you really believe he does not know your secret intents and agendas?

You may be the one that God wants to use as a <u>vessel</u> to save a sinner just like me.

(1) **VESSEL**- a person into whom some quality (as grace) is infused: a child of light, a true vessel of the Lord- H.S. Laski

1 Timothy 1:12- 13) I think Christ Jesus our Lord, who has given me strength, that he considered me faithful, appointing me to his service. 13) Even though I was a blasphemer and a persecutor and a violent man, I was shown mercy because I acted in ignorance and unbelief.

The idea of service and ministry is greatly misunderstood these days. All believers are in the ministry and service as a child of God. Every believer has some service to perform for the Lord.

Please Lord I pray you use me as your vessel to share your words of love in a creative powerful way.

You may be the one that God wants to use as a vessel to save a <u>sinner</u> just like me.

(2) **SINNER- a vitiated (to make faulty or defective) state of human nature in which the self is estranged from God**

Before I could identify myself as a sinner I had to know just what a sin was and was not. In the definition above, state of nature in the self is estranged from God.

What does this mean?

Here are the questions I had to answer honestly and accept the answers in order for me to understand that I am a sinner.

HAVE YOU EVER TOLD A LIE?

ANSWER: EVER? OF COURSE I HAVE!

WHAT DOES THAT MAKE YOU?

ANSWER: I GUESS IT WOULD MAKE ME A LIAR?

HAVE YOU EVER STOLEN ANYTHING IN YOUR LIFE?

ANSWER: THAT IS A HARD ONE TO ANSWER, BUT YES I HAVE.

WHAT DOES THAT MAKE YOU?

ANSWER: A THIEF?

QUESTION: HAVE YOU EVER LUSTED FOR ANYONE YOU LAID YOUR EYES ON?

ANSWER: I AM SURE THAT I HAVE, OKAY, YES I HAVE!

WHAT DOES THAT MAKE YOU?

ANSWER: I AM NOT SURE TO TELL YOU THE TRUTH.

IT MAKES YOU AN ADULTRESS.

HAVE YOU EVER USED THE LORD'S NAME IN VEIN?

ANSWER: YES

WHAT DOES THAT MAKE YOU?

ANSWER: I DO NOT KNOW

A BLASPHEMER

QUESTION FROM ME: WHAT DOES BLASPHEMER MEAN?

ANSWER FROM PERSON: ONE WHO SPEAKS DISRESPECTFULLY OF SACRED THINGS.

SO HAVE YOU EVER SINNED?

ANSWER: YES MOST ASSUREDLY I HAVE.

SO WHAT DOES THAT MAKE YOU?

ANSWER: A SINNER!

SO ON JUDGMENT DAY, DO YOU FEEL YOU WILL GO TO HEAVEN OR HELL?

ANSWER: HELL?

IS THAT OKAY WITH YOU?

ANSWER: NO, I DO NOT THINK THAT IT IS.

SO IF YOU HAVE ALREADY BROKEN THE LAWS OF GOD, HOW CAN YOU GO TO HEAVEN?

ANSWER: I DO NOT KNOW. MAYBE IF I AM GOOD PERSON AND TRY NOT TO DO THESE THINGS AGAIN.

WELL THE TRUTH IS I AM A SINNER AND GOD WILL NOT JUST PRETEND THAT I HAVE NOT ALREADY COMMITTED THESE SINS LIKE I HAVE IN THE PAST.

OH MY GOD, HOW CAN I MAKE THEM GO AWAY?

Romans Road of Scripture

I. Romans 3:10- as is written: "There is no one righteous, not even one":

II. Romans 3:23- for all have sinned, and come short of the Glory of God.

III. Romans 5:8- but God demonstrates his own love for us this: While we were still sinners, Christ died for us.

IV. Romans 5:12- Therefore, just as sin entered the world through one man, and death through sin, and in this way death came to all men, because all sinned

V. Romans 6:23- For the wages of sin is death, but the gift of God is eternal life in Christ Jesus our Lord.

VI. Romans 10: 9-11- That if thou shalt confess with your mouth "Jesus is Lord," and believe in your heart that God raised him from the dead, you will be saved. For it is with your heart that you believe in and are justified, and it is with your mouth that you confess and are saved. As the scripture says, "Anyone who trusts him will never be put to shame."

VII. Romans 10:13- for "Everyone who calls on the name of the Lord will be saved."

VIII. Romans 10:17- Consequently, faith comes from hearing the message, and the message is heard through the word of Christ.

Yes the divorce was a <u>devastating</u> time for all involved, but the reality is that at the age of twelve I would never have become an alcoholic if I had not put the bottle to my lips and ingested it.

DEVASTING: Devastate- **<u>to lay waste</u>**, as by war, fire, flood etc. make desolate; ravage.

Lay waste- Do you know the true meaning of those words? I did not. So I was driven to find out for my own knowledge and after I examined it I needed and wanted to share it with you. First I will take the word Lay and define it.

Lay: to place or put; especially to cause to be in specified place, state, or condition.

Next I looked up waste.

Waste: To use or expend thoughtlessly, uselessly, or without return;

Devastation is a true condition that we all will experience at different times in our lives. However it is not meant to be a staple in life.

Is it a staple in your life? _____

It sure was in mine. So I needed to look into why?

When I looked at the definition of the word **lay,** again I noticed that I had something to do with my own state and condition. Then when I added the definition of the word **waste** I was shocked. I would constantly expend my feelings and emotions thoughtlessly, uselessly and in most cases without any positive return. Now I needed to find out why and how to change that.

NAHUM 1:7 the Lord is good, a strong hold in the day of trouble; and he knoweth them that trust in him.

"The Lord is good "people and I now feel wonderful in knowing that. I do not know you, where come from or what your circumstances are, but I do know God loves you and he wants to save you. "A strong hold in the day of trouble," Do you want to get to a good shelter? The Lord is the shelter you need. "And he knoweth them that trust in him." I longer have to feel lost in the shuffle of family, husband, work and the rest of the world.

Here is a huge clue that got me thinking! If you are not saved, the answer is quite simple. It is because you will not come to Him, for He can save you and He will save you if you genuinely ask him to.

I read this verse before I understood what the truth was, but I instinctively knew that the truth lay within it. I was going to go forward and soften my heart to find out just what the truth was. I had nothing to lose except my miserable self.

Whatever it maybe that has you or a loved one handcuffed to it has <u>seduced</u> you into captivity, many things certainly seduced me into captivity throughout my life.

SEDUCE- to lead astray! <u>Entice</u> into wrong doing or believe: disloyalty

Seduction, Oh just the sound of the word is enticing. I know it well from both sides of the fence. Most people's first thought of the word seduction would be a physical type of seduction, but there is so much more to this word for me. People, places and things had no problem seducing me and I received an incredible high from playing the seduction game with all those things.

What is seducing you or better yet what are you seducing? _____

1 John 2:26 (NIV) I am writing these things to you about those who are trying to lead you astray.

Seduce means to lead from the truth. The word seduce in this verse is fantastic because the truth is; I was always seduced by mental, spiritual adultery or self-destruction. Where ever your mind goes your heart and body are soon to follow!

I never knew about that invisible line, but when I crossed it my needs and wants turned into the handcuffs that shackled me from the <u>freedom </u> to live a free full life of truth.

FREEDOM -The condition of being personally free in liberty-from bondage or slavery**.**

I grow up in what some may call the Hippie era so freedom was a big word that carried a lot of power. I lived in New Hampshire where the license plates logo was "Live Free or Die." Today as I look back on it I think a large part of my generation should have had that license plate read, "Live Free to Die."

We fought for the freedom to find ourselves, and lost the whole world in the search.

We fought for the freedom of sex and have a world full of sexual transmitted diseases that are killing our youth.

We fought for the freedom of expression and have a world of fowl mouth youth that have no idea how to communicate in a real language.

We fought for the freedom to do alcohol and drugs and have a world full of addicts that die for their freedom to continue to do them. I know I would have!

We fought for the freedom to live together out of marriage and we have a world full of divorce and one parent families.

Here again we see that freedom is also a condition, a condition that carries the responsibility of having to live with the consequence in the future. I was not free I lived in bondage to all things that seduced me or that I had managed to seduce for me.

Romans 6:19-21 (NIV) 19) I put this in human terms because you are weak in your natural selves. Just as you used to offer the parts of your body in slavery to impurity and to ever increasing wickedness, so now offer them in slavery to righteousness leading to holiness. 20) When you were slaves to sin, you were free from the control of righteousness. 21) What benefit did you reap at that time from the things you are now ashamed of? Those result in death!

In verse 19 Paul says "I put this in human terms." He is not speaking by inspiration he is speaking in a manner that we will understand. Observe the tragedy of our young who have rebelled against the rules and regulations of the establishment and who have been destroyed by the thousands by drugs and alcohol! You may be delivered from one group its rules and regulations, but if you don't turn to Christ, **you may be going from the frying pan to the fire. The Lord Jesus says when you commit sin, you are the servant of sin.**

John 8:32 Then you will know the truth and the truth will set you free

The truth will set you free. The truth is that Jesus Christ is the savior of the world.

HE IS TRUTH! HE IS YOUR FREEDOM!

First I came to know him as my savior. Then as I went on with him I learned by experience that I was free. I was free from the penalty of sin. He doesn't even ask us to live a Christian life. He asks us to trust Him and let Him live his life through us. When we yield to Him, we are TRULY free.

Nor did they follow through with the promises they had made to me in the <u>fantasy</u> state of the relationship.

    (1) FANTASY- a creation of the imaginative faculty whether expressed or merely conceived as a fanciful design or invention, a chimerical (existing only as the product of unchecked imagination) or fantastic notion.

Ecclesiastes 5:7 (The Message) but against all illusion and <u>fantasy</u> and empty talk there's always this rock foundation: Fear God!

Oh God, why do you want me to fear you? I fear so many things already.

    For the unbeliever, the fear of God is the fear of his judgment and judgment to come.

    For the believer, the fear of God is something much different. Passionate believers are not to be scared of God. We have no reason to be afraid of Him. We have His promise that nothing can separate us from his love. We have His promise that He will never leave us. Fearing God means having such a reverence for Him that it has a great impact on the way we live our lives. The fear of God is respecting Him, obeying him, submitting to His discipline, and worshipping Him in awe.

The decision was made so I could escape the <u>guidance</u> of my parents.

    (1) Guidance: The direction provide by a guide

How could I listen to a guide when I thought I knew it all, and I did not want to be a goody, goody?

Ezekiel 5:7 "Therefore this is what God, the Master, says: You've been more headstrong and willful than any of the nations around you, refusing my guidance, ignoring my directions. You've sunk to the gutter level of those around you.

How true for me. But in my defense I truly believed that God was just the judge and the punisher. God made us and he knows precisely what we need. The best advice I have ever received in my life is the advice I received straight from the Lord in his Word. Guidance is an act of guiding you my friends, not controlling you. The old reasoning that he would take away my control was a real stumbling block for me in my life. Do not allow it to be your stumbling block! Always remember that when guidance is offered to you it will always be your choice to follow through with it or not.

Hopefully if not now soon you will have a relationship with the Lord and you will instinctively with prayer know the guidance that is right for you.

The Bible and Jesus scared me to death because I thought they would take away my freedom to do the things I wanted to do. That is not the case. I have found that the Bible and a true relationship with Jesus have given me the guidance I have always needed. I simply had to take as much interest in them as I did in trying to survive in my earlier years.

God is the best Father I could have ever asked for! I do not deserve him, but through the blood of Jesus Christ he loves me anyways and we show each other every day.

The decision was made so I could escape the guidance of my <u>parents.</u>

(2)   **Parents**: one that begets or brings forth offspring: a person that brings up and cares for another.

2Timothy 3:2 People will be lovers of themselves, lovers of money, boastful, proud, abusive, disobedient to their parents, ungrateful, unholy

Does this not describe our country today? Why do we feel that we are "all that?"

Here is a good one for you. Have you ever heard anyone ask after a person dies, whether that person was rich or poor?

"How much did they leave?"

Here is the universal and correct answer that no one ever says EVERYTHING!

We take no worldly things with us when we leave, and it does not matter where we are going, we still take nothing.

Parents please start storing up your treasures in heaven by showing your children where their true inheritance is, in heaven. And children embrace the love of your sovereign Father, God!

The honest and real problem with these marriages was that I did not give myself and these men the time for to get to know each other and because of our inpatients we had no idea if we were compatible for the <u>covenant of marriage.</u>

COVENANT OF MARRIAGE: The state of being sanctified; holiness; Sacredness; solemnity

MARRIAGE- the state of being united to a person of the opposite sex as husband or wife in a consensual and contractual relationship recognized by law

These words covenant and marriage were used in my testimony describing five of my marriages. Not what my marriages were, but what they were not.

Matthew 19:11_(The Message) But Jesus said, "Not everyone is mature enough to live a married life. It requires a certain aptitude and grace. Marriage isn't for everyone. Some, from birth seemingly, never give marriage a thought. Others never get asked—or accepted. And some decide not to get married for kingdom reasons. But if you're capable of growing into the largeness of marriage, do it."

Maturity in faith is an essential in the covenant of marriage. I had no faith therefore I had no maturity or clue of what my vows meant.

Malachi 2:13 (The Message) and here's a second offense: You fill the place of worship with your whining and sniveling because you don't get what you want from God. Do you know why? Simple, Because God was there as a witness when you spoke your marriage vows to your young bride, and now you've broken those vows, broken the faith-bond with your vowed companion, your covenant wife. God, not you, made marriage. His Spirit inhabits even the smallest details of marriage. And what does he want from marriage? Children of God, that's what. So guard the spirit of marriage within you. Don't cheat on your spouse.

These verses are regarding men that have divorced their wife's for foreign girls and then they came to the same altar where their wife's shed their tears and the men would try to make their offerings. God pays no attention to those offerings; you would do just as well to just stay away.

Ladies and gentlemen if you break your covenant of marriage and try to cover it up with service and good will, (alimony, child support, service at church) He will not accept your service. He knows your hypocrisy. God heard the vows you made to your mate and yes those vows were a promise made to Him also. In every divorce someone or both have sinned and Satan has gotten his way.

My <u>challenges</u> in life were many, some of which I got myself into through making wrong choices, some out of immature ignorance, others out of outside pressures and some out of just plain selfishness and rebellion.

(1) CHALLENGES- calling into account or into question

James 1:2 (The Message) Consider it a sheer gift, friends, when tests and <u>challenges</u> come at you from all sides. You know that under pressure, your faith-life is forced into the open and shows its true colors. So don't try to get out of anything prematurely. Let it do its work so you become mature and well-developed, not deficient in any way.

James is telling us here that God does not give us trouble for trouble's sake, it is not the end. We are told that we are to rejoice and count it all joy, that God is testing us his way. I totally understand how absurd this sounds to some, me included. One question that is asked over and over again is, "Whether the Christian is to experience joy in the mix of all the trials and stresses of life." Well the answer is an in vatic NO!

That is not what James is conveying here. You should not say that you are reconciled to the will of God in your troubles when you are not. That is not reality, my friend when you are not reconciled. You are not reconciled until you can rejoice, and that is not always easy and in most cases takes time, trust and faith and most of all prayer and resolution. Without troubles in life we would never grow, learn and come to trust that we will never be given more than we can handle when in a true relationship with Jesus.

My challenges in life were many, some of which I got myself into through making wrong choices, some out of immature ignorance, others out of outside pressures and some out of just plain <u>selfishness </u> and rebellion.

(2) **SELFISHNESS –** the characteristic of being selfish; caring chiefly for oneself, for one's own Interest or comfort: UNDUE LOVE FOR SELF!

I was told that I was selfish although I never saw myself that way. I absolutely was self-centered but not willing to say selfish. Let me throw this at you for thought. If you are someone like I was and you are constantly in a survival mode with no tools of how to survive and it is not even clear what you are trying to survive from. There were even times that I was not sure if I even wanted to survive.

There is a thin line between selfishness and the need to survive. However I have found in time that both are needless feelings that have nothing to do with love, life or anything good.

Cast your eyes unto the Lord! He will plant the seed and if you care for Him and your love for Him is shared in all that you do, your fruit will be bountiful. You will not keep what you do not give it away! If you fight the Devil's feelings of selfishness and plant your seeds of God all through your life you will never have to feel the need to survive again, of God all through your life you will never have to feel the need to survive again, your fruits will be bountiful.

God keeps my basket full of surprises constantly when I am full of the spirit and allowing Him to reveal His word to me. Some of these are the things I have wanted my whole life and I am jubilant when I receive them. Others remind me of those gifts from grandmother on my birthday or Christmas that where couched in a big box, wrapped beautifully and decorated with an elaborate bow. My selfishness and greed told me that the gift inside was going to be the greatest thing ever. So I would go at that gift as if my life depended on it by tearing of the beautiful paper and bow not even noticing or caring about the beauty of the outer wrapping. I then popped open that box cover and there it was, a hand knitted sweater that shocked me with its ugliness.

That ugliness however was my own distorted worldly perception. This sweater was a labor of love that was made and designed just for me. My grandmother was the creator and she knew just how it would look on me. She also knew the day would come that I would desperately need this sweater to protect me from the cold. No this sweater was not what I thought I wanted, but it was something that I would need and yes it kept me warm when I needed it.

As I matured and I no longer had that incredible labor of love to wrap my cold body in, the memories of that immeasurable labor of love will warm me forever!

God has a wonderful way of disguising some of the gifts he gives us. Some of these gifts are wrapped in what we consider very ugly wrapping and because we do not like the wrapping we take that gift and store it somewhere pretending we never received it. The problem with storing this gift away by sitting it on the shelf in your mind is that it will take up space needed for other things; you will continue to wonder what it is and the day will come if only out of curiosity when you will have to find out what it is.

One of God gifts delivered to me a few days after my father's passing away was wrapped in one of the ugliest papers any of us could image. There is not a person on this earth that does not dread the thought of being told they have cancer.

When I was diagnosed not too long ago with breast cancer I was devastated! I will share more about this journey with God in a future God's Emergency Room. But for now know that I found out that cancer was only the ugly wrapping. The gifts I received from The Lord because of the cancer were wrapped so deeply inside that ugly "C" word wrapping that it took me time to find the life changing gifts inside my journey.

One of the gifts wrapped so deeply in that ugly wrapping was that I no longer had to fear this thing that I could not understand, because the Lord had me wrapped so tightly in His sweater of love, to keep me warm and safe.

Galatians 5:16-18 (The Message) my counsel is this: Live freely, animated and motivated by God's Spirit. Then you won't feed the compulsions of selfishness. For there is a root of sinful self-interest in us that is at odds with a free spirit, just as the free spirit is incompatible with <u>selfishness</u>. These two ways of life are antithetical, so that you cannot live at times one way and at times another way according to how you feel on any given day. Why don't you choose to be led by the Spirit and so escape the erratic compulsions of a law-dominated existence?

The translation of these verses is that we as humans will live by selfishness and compulsions of the flesh and or the Spirit. The flesh and the Spirit are contrary to each other. It is very important to see that the flesh fights the Spirit and the Spirit fights the flesh.

A believer has a new nature, one that is born of the Spirit. You will still have the old nature of the flesh, and will continue to as long as you are here on this earth. The thought that the old nature will pick up and move is a tragic mistake. There are those that question whether they are walking within the flesh or the Spirit. Do not kid yourself about this. You can know and will know when you are, or are not walking with the Spirit.

There are times when I am walking in the selfishness of the flesh and I may choose not to change it right away. But the Spirit always makes me aware of it. These are the time when my old nature wants to wander away from the Lord and He allows me to do it.

Have you experienced this?_____

On the other side of the spectrum there are times when the Spirit is in me so strong that I cry out how blessed I am the God brings me to a higher plain.

Galatians 6:7-8 don't be misled: No one makes a fool of God. What a person plants, he will harvest. The person who plants <u>selfishness</u>, ignoring the needs of others—ignoring God!—harvests a crop of weeds. All he'll have to show for his life is weeds! But the one who plants in response to God, letting God's Spirit do the growth work in him, harvests a crop of real life, eternal life.

This is the immutable law the guides all things in life. It is taught, should be heard, and taken seriously that when you plant corn, you get corn; if you sow cotton you get cotton. God says you will not get by with sin. It does not matter how many pills you take, or how much you do or do not get involved with the insanity and selfishness of the world; God says you will not get by with sin.

God says you will reap what you sow and God will not be mocked! If you sow selfish, self-serving behavior, that is what your harvest will reap.

Reaping "life everlasting" blesses you with the fruit of the Spirit in this life and the glorious prospect of the future.

The list includes but is not limited to rape, unfaithful husbands, premature birth of a son, alcoholic husband, being a single mother, signing over custody of my son that I loved more than life itself to his father, alienating parts of my family in an unhealthy way, child molestation, and living every single day of my life with <u>anxiety</u> and panic.

(1) **ANXIETY**_–a tense and **emotional state** characterized by **fear** and **apprehension**.

FEAR, OH MY LORD! As strong a word as fear is, it does not come close to describing the demoralizing ugly monster named anxiety. Sorry, but apprehension will not fly with me either, although I will totally agree that it is and emotional state.

Allow me to give a description of anxiety and panic that comes directly from one that it devoured and tried to murder in the slowest most heinous way conceivable. It is Satan at his best. After much thought of how to describe this murder of life and how it emotionally and physically cripples those of us that experience it. The following parable is the best I could humanly conjure up, and believe me it still falls way short.

Close your eyes and imagine being buried under six feet of tightly packed soil that cover every inch of your body including your mouth and nose. In your mouth is a small cocktail straw to breath but you cannot get a full breath. The soil is packed so tight around you that you are sure it will crush your chest and every bone in your body.

Your head is telling you to just let go and die that moment. But your fear of what death is keeps you fighting. For what you have no idea. Your loved ones want to help you put have no understanding that they cannot dig you out!

I hope you were able to get that picture in your head and heart and imagine the feelings and emotions going through such a thing. Now I would like you to multiply those feelings and thoughts by one thousand and you now have a full blown panic attack.

This word anxiety and the word panic following it ran my life or lack of it. It consumed my inner soul and every aspect of my life for many years. The anxiety of everything, or nothing at all, would always be the beginning of a journey down a very dark path, followed by a panic attack that would lead me to a dead end.

How trapped we feel when this demoralizing, agonizing, attack hits with no warning, no reason, and gives you now idea how long it is going to stay.

The feelings of anxiety and panic are experienced by people all through the Bible and in every case the cause is lack of true faith and trust in the Lord.

1Peter 5:7- cast all your anxiety on him because He cares for you.

"He cares for you, literally means that you matter to him. In the verse Peter is talking about anxiety. The Lord Jesus said, "Come unto Me all ye that labor and are heavy laden, and I will rest you" (see Matt. 11:28). Paul told the Philippians believers, "Worry about nothing; pray about everything." That means take it to the Lord in prayer, and leave it there. "DO NOT PICK IT UP AGAIN!

"Trust also in Him; and He shall bring it to pass." Give God time. He will work things out in your life. God is good; forget the heathen concept that God is a terrible being. Many Christians view God that way. They think of Him as some sort of villain who will turn on you at any moment.

He NEVER will- He is your FATHER! He wants to SAVE you, but you must commit your way to him. If you have been taught or are being taught by anyone that God will turn on you, run from them as fast as you can!

(2) **PANIC**- a sudden unreasonable, overpowering fear

Psalm 37: 7- (NIV) be still before the Lord and wait patiently for him; do not fret when men succeed in their ways, when they carry out their wicked schemes.

Be still before the Lord, How hard is that?

Very!

Wait patiently? OK I get it. Seems impossible doesn't it? I thought it was, but here is something that I was told to try and surprisingly found that worked. In the middle of an attack I decided to pray to the Lord, not to stop the panic but to give me the patients and faith that he could and would help me. He heard me!

Romans 8:14 (The Message) for you did not receive a spirit that makes you a slave again to fear, but you receive the spirit of son ship

You may not understand what this verse is saying to you, I sure didn't. Here is an explanation. God does not drive his sheep he leads them. When the Lord told of the safety of his sheep, He made it clear that they were not forced into the will of His hand and that of the Father. He said "my sheep hear my voice, and I know them and they follow me" **(John 10:27).**

The sound of this was music to my ears and a light in my heart. All forms or earthly things had driven me down the wrong path for so many years. It had been my addictions, relationships, money, material things, and anything that owned me and played a big part in my panic. THAT WAS GOING TO STOP!

Through all these situations I was very comfortable in the position of being the victim, because that way I never had to take <u>responsibility</u> for my part in the choices I made or situations I got myself into.

RESPONSIBILITY the state of being responsible or <u>accountable;</u> <u>capable</u> of being accounted for

John 9:41 (The Message) Jesus said, "If you were really blind, you would be blameless, but since you claim to see everything so well, you're <u>accountable</u> for every fault and failure."

The verses preceding this verse began with a blind man that had been healed, so he saw both physically and spiritually. We end up with this verse dealing with religious rulers who were very tragically spiritually blind, yet who thought they could see.

They said they were sin free, in the presence of Christ, in the presence of the light and in the revelation of God.

Some of the most dogmatic (characterized by or given to the expression of opinions very strongly or positively as if they were facts) people today are the atheist and the cultist. They say they see, but they are blind. They reject the Lord Jesus Christ, so their sins remain. They may have twenty-twenty vision but they are blind.

One morning on television I heard Pastor Mathew Hagee say that the word responsible should be looked at this way. Response- Able, hearing that was as if he had hit me with a two by four on the side of my head, was I truly just not able all these years? I knew that I was capable but was I able? NO! Why, because I did nothing through the Lord and he is our only power.

Proverbs 22:17-21 Listen carefully to my wisdom; take to heart what I can teach you. You'll treasure its sweetness deep within; you'll give it bold expression in your speech. To make sure your foundation is trust in God, I'm laying it all out right now just for you. I'm giving you thirty sterling principles— tested guidelines to live by. Believe me—these are truths that work, and will keep you accountable to those who sent you.

EVIL- I am in no way excusing the <u>evil</u> part that other people may take in our life's tragedies and wrong doings.

All evil is sin and all sin is evil!

Who is Satan?

Revelation 12:9-The great dragon was hurled down- that ancient serpent called the devil, or Satan, who <u>leads the whole world astray.</u> He was hurled to the earth, and his angels with him.

Satan - the rebellious angel who in Christian belief is the adversary of God and lord of evil

Most people when they think of Satan believe that he is hideous and grotesque in his appearance. This is not the case. The Bible tells us Satan is a fallen angel of the highest order, created in perfection in all his ways. Paul writes that Satan transforms himself into "an angle of light". Therefore, if we saw Satan, he might well be the most beautiful creature we have ever seen, if God permitted him to reveal himself. Satan is limited in what he can and cannot do. His power is limited in scope; however his power is more than we could comprehend in our mortal being.

We know about Satan through the revelation of scripture.

(1) He was the seal of perfection full of wisdom and beauty

(2) He was in the Garden of Eden before the fall

(3) He was the anointed covering cherub

(4) He was perfect

(5) His heart was lifted up because of his beauty

Satan was not created fallen, but with the ability to choose "free will." He along with the rest of the angels could choose the worship God or not. Cherub angels stand in the presence of God, before the throne of God. He along with one third of the other angels chose to reject God.

What was the cause of Satan's fall?

It was his pride, he rejoiced in his beauty, forsaking the wisdom he had been created with.

Mathew 16:23 - Jesus turned and said to Peter, "Get behind me, Satan! You are a stumbling block to me; you do not have in mind the things of God, but the things of men."

It is Satanic for anyone to deny the facts of the gospel which are that Jesus died on the cross for our sins, was buried, and rose again from the dead. The death of Christ is the only thing that can save us, my friend.

Imagine this: Here is Peter by whom the Spirit of God could say that Jesus was the Son of God, and yet he could in the next moment let Satan deceive him! Do not for one minute think Satan is not real!

I did not know that I was not the <u>axis of the earth</u> and everything on or in it.

AXIS OF THE EARTH - the planet on which man dwells: also the people who inhabit it.

Axis- The central line about which the parts of a body or thing are regularly arranged

Genesis 1:1 in the beginning God created the heaven and the EARTH.

This is one of the most profound statements ever made, and yet we find a way to challenge it in this age we live in. However brief, this verse is the doorway through which you will have to walk into the Bible.

This was written many years ago by Vernon J McGee.

My friend, in the midst of all the unbelief, the hostility toward God which is around us today, the greatest thing you can do as a human being is to publicly choose the Lord Jesus Christ. To believe in God the Father Almighty, the maker of heaven and earth and to receive His Son, Jesus Christ, is the most glorious privilege that you and I can have. We hear a lot of talk about freedom of speech and freedom of every sort, but this poor crowd around us who talks so loudly of freedom, doesn't seem to know what freedom really is. We have real freedom when we choose Jesus Christ as our savior.

I need for all of you that are reading this to understand that nothing I was doing or experiencing was that much out of the ordinary according to this <u>morally </u>challenge world of ours.

Moral-of or relating to principles of right and wrong in behave

Proverbs 11:5- Moral characters makes for smooth traveling; an evil life is a hard life.

Come on brothers and sisters we know what is right and what is wrong. Sure we can all put a spin on anything we want to do, but you cannot deny that in your heart you know the truth. Moral simply means right!

DIAGNOSES

I had some good things happen in my life. I got sober from alcohol at the age of thirty, I had a wonderful son, gave birth to a daughter in sobriety, I got my education, and accepted what I called a **higher power** into my life.

HIGHER POWER-

HIGHER – superior, lofty or exalted in quality, character, rank, kind etc.

POWER- The right, ability, or capacity to exercise control; legal authority capacity or competency.

When the good Lord decided that it was time for me to come out of the entanglement of my alcohol addiction twenty five years ago I accepted Him only as my Higher Power. I thought that just believing in a power greater than myself, even if it had no identity was a stretch of the imagination and it was.

In time I accepted the fact that it was God, but I was unable to allow myself to accept Jesus was anything other than a hippie and a rebel of his time.

I was gifted sobriety in a twelve step program, unknown to me until just recently that the program was structured around the Bible. But because of people like me that would not surrender to the truth, the originators had to change the program to be more generic with no mention of the Bible, God or Jesus.

The time came when God decided that it was the correct time for me to finish the higher power thing and find the truth. Of course he had to bring me to my knees before I would even acknowledge what He wanted me to know and in future God Emergency Room text, I will share those storms with you.

John 14:6 (NIV) Jesus answered, "I am the way and the truth and the life. No one comes to the Father except though me.

Pay close attention to this verse. No church or ceremony can bring you to God. Only Christ can bring you to God, either you have Christ or you don't have him; either you trust Him or you don't.

He is the source of life.

<u>REVELATION</u> 21:6 He said to me: It is done. I am the Alpha and the Omega, the beginning and the end. To him who is thirsty I will give drink without cost from the spring of the water of life.

The speaker here is The Lord Jesus Christ. Without a true relationship with him I have no rights, abilities, or control it is all only an illusion.

He is the Alpha and the Omega!

Alpha –the first letter of the Greek alphabet; a name applied to Christ. **Revelation 1:8, 22:13,**

Omega- the last letter of the Greek alphabet, a name applied to Christ. **Revelation 1:8, 21:6, 22:13**

Not God or <u>**Jesus**</u> just a higher power.

JESUS- When Jesus came to this world the first time he was sent as a **savior**. The second time He comes (no one knows when that will be), He will be a **judge**. It is made clear here that Christ at this time is not condemning anyone, but those that are not in Christ are already condemned.

Many people say that the world is on trial today. That is not the truth! The world is already LOST and that is the world we live in today. I know that I live **<u>in</u>** this world, but I do not have to live **<u>of</u>** this world.

Romans 8:1 (NIV) 1) Therefore there is no condemnation for those who are in Christ Jesus, 2) because through Christ Jesus the law of the Spirit of life set me free from the law of sin and death.

Here is an explanation of these truths that I was blessed with and could comprehend and understand. When we are non-believers we are just like a person who is in prison on deaths row and we are being asked if they will accept a pardon. Of course the person in prison would say YES with gratitude.

Will you or I? _____

Life Through the Spirit

That pardon for us is in the words of the Gospel and will reveal to us that God sent his only Son to die for our sins. When Jesus died on the cross he died for all of us that believe in Him as our Savior. Good works does not get you to Heaven!

This is not telling us that I am on trial, because as a non-believer I am already condemned in prison and waiting execution. No wonder I always felt the way I did about life. The Gospel is to save those that are already lost.

Are you lost? _____

Rats always run to the darkest corner when the light enters the room. I was a rat!

I pray that you will continue to follow my journey in finding the truth!

You will be amazed at the things God reveals to me and the way he does it. I continue to go through all kinds of twist and turns, rebellion, surrender and I would never take any part of it back.

Please pray with me?

Being a Christian is having a relationship with God! Relationships require communication. The way to communicate with God our Father is thru prayer, God knows our hearts and minds but he wants to hear from us. He wants us to talk to Him and for us to look to Him and His word for guidance.

How to Pray

I had heard about prayer but I thought there were right ways and a wrong ways to do it. I felt that I was not eloquent enough with my words to pray to him especially out loud. We all face obstacles in life, among them are illness, grief, disappointment, failure, anger, fear, addiction, divorce, sorrow, and a sense of despair about the state of our world. We are all busy doing something or nothing at all and stress is all around us.

Even the disciples said; "Lord teach us to pray."

Jesus did just that through his example of how to pray.

The Lord's Prayer is found in **Matthew 6:9-13.**

Now I will not even try to tell you that I had never learned or said the Lord's Prayer before in my life. I must have said it hundreds or thousands of times. Every twelve step program I attended always closed with the Lord's Prayer but I never considered the true meaning of the words I was speaking, nor did I understand what they meant. Below is an interpretation given to me by my dear friend, sister in Christ and accountability partner, Elizabeth Choike.

The Lord's Prayer

Our Father: Lord, help me to remember that you are my Father, a caring parent who will love me and protect me much more than any human parent.

Who art in heaven: Heaven is your home, Lord and thank you for letting me see glimmers of heaven every day here on earth, in sunrise and sunset, in thunder, lightning and rain bearing clouds, in oceans with their rippling waves and tides. In the rivers that flow into the ocean, in roses, daisies and snowflakes.

Hallowed be thy name: Father let me honor your name in my every word, action and thought.

Thy kingdom come; Let me remember, dear God, that this world is only temporary, that your glorious kingdom will indeed come and I long to be swept up into it.

Thy will be done, on earth as it is in heaven: Father, in this world, we are often so far from doing your will as Jesus revealed it. Help me to live my life according to your will and help make earth more like heaven.

Give us this day our daily bread: God of abundance, thank you for providing so generously all that I need. Remind me to share what you provide for me so that all may have their daily bread.

And forgive us our trespasses: Without your continuous forgiveness, Lord, where would I be?

As we forgive those who trespass against us: I should be more forgiving Lord, show me how.

And lead us not into temptation: Father, I often feel that I am being tried. Help me to remember that my small trials are nothing compared to those of your Son, my brother, and give me the strength and faith to persevere.

But deliver us from evil: Dear God, intervene for me because I am weak, and without your deliverance I am like a lost and wondering child. Draw me safely into your protective embrace, Lord.

Amen: You, Father, are the final amen, the way, the truth, the life.

God just wants to hear from us, just talk to him. He is your Father; you can share anything with him.

"God's Emergency Room" is not a onetime shot from God having me share my experiences and revelations. It is a series of work books where I will share all kinds of feelings, emotions, rebellion, sins, and my entire journey of many trips to His emergency room and the prescriptions given to me through His words for my healing.

Up and coming work books (God willing) for "GOD'S EMERGENCY ROOM"

(1) **WHY DOES THIS LIFE HURT? SO BAD!** My life was castrated by fear, anxiety and emptiness. My life may have looked great to outsiders but it was all just smoke and mirrors. (published)

(2) HERE IS THE CHURCH, HERE IS THE STEEPLE: Is an amazing middle of the night journey for me a person that had converted to Judaism years prior, now looking for answers to life and ending up at a church in the wee hours of this mystical night. This night was the night God planted His seed of Faith in my heart. Without my permission or knowledge.

(3) **DOCTORS OR GOD? HOSPITALS OR CHURCH?** I was more comfortable in emergency rooms or at home than anywhere else in this world. But it was now time for me to revisit the church that was part of that mystical night. This was not a clear decision for me; as a matter of fact it was downright painful. But my curiosity was getting the best of me and I could no longer deny the intervention that God had walked me through at that church so recently. It would have been easier for me to go to the hospital and get a shot to stop my insanity than it would be to go meet what I thought was going to be these religious people.

(4) **PASTOR, OR PASS IT BY?** This is a not so flattering story about how I felt and what I thought of the word of God and what the practice of religion was all about. God however found that it was time for me to learn faith and the truth of God being my Father was not about religion, it was about a relationship with Him and until I faced my ignorance's and prejudice and went to talk to the Pastor I would continue to live in the dark.

(5) **NAH, NAH, YOU DON'T HAVE CONTR0L!** oHow difficult it is to accept the fact that we are not in control. God takes me through a life changing journey and reveals to me that I can let go of my old ways and he was going to prove it to me. I think he probably laughed his way through convincing me because I was not easy, but I was learning that he loved me anyway!

(6) **CHASTISE OR BAPTIZE?** This is a work book that describes and brings you through what may sound at times laughable to those that live in faith. But it was a very tough decision for me to make on whether I was going to go on feeling chastised because of my disobediences to all or if I was going to show surrender and take a shot at obedience and surrender to be Baptized.

(7) **WILL YOU STILL LOVE ME IN THE MORNING?** erHere I share with you how after I had been Saved and Baptized and I really wanted to be the woman God wanted me to be. Gambling however was still the most powerful influence in my life and I thought that I would be punished for my sins. Like every lesson this one has twist and turns that some may not believe.

(8) **DO NOT TURN OFF YOUR HEARING AID!** The horror of the sickness of the man I loved most on earth, my father, is in this lesson. I will also share with you my selfishness that came with the fear of death and everything that comes with it. This is the story of the beginning of me realizing that I needed to stop making excuses for my life and start being silent and listen to what was being revealed to me.

(9) **MAY I RETURN THIS GIFT YOU HAVE GIVEN ME?** The day after my father's death something was telling me to get my left breast checked. I was hundreds of miles away from home and grieving my father's passing, this was crazy. The day after that it felt as though someone was gently touching my breast. One of my biggest fears in the world was now going to be faced head on, I had breast cancer.

(10) **WHY ME? WHY NOT ME?** After my diagnoses I was so mad at God! I was incensed and at the beginning not able to understand what I had done wrong. In this book I am sharing with you how I express things that most would not dare express never mind share with others because of the fear of God. But he has given me the strength to share with all that want to know.

(11) **CANCER OR GOD?** It was now time for me to make a choice on what I was going to live for, or die for. This title says it all.

(12) **WHAT DO YOU MEAN YOU WANT A DIVORSE?** I am going through cancer and we have a covenant!

There will be future emergencies to follow because we are either in an emergency, coming out of emergency, or in between emergencies. God Bless all of you!

About the Author

Kim Bernasconi is a woman that could have been characterized as a sober alcoholic, a woman that has fought through five marriages and divorces, a rebel to authority, a materialistic glutton, a self-centered but not selfish person, one that must have control, but never did, some may say a Diva, someone that has always denied the Bible, Jesus and anyone or anything that was connected to those truths and this description would not have been a false one in the judgments of the human flesh.

However God saw her as one of his daughter's. She may have been one of his weakest lambs, but through His tough but fair love he was able to reach her and introduce her to her Savior, Jesus Christ.

Kim has since accepted Jesus as her Lord, her God, and her savior and surrendered to the truth that she is not in control and no longer wants to be. She is transparent in the fact that she works daily on her flesh driven character defects with the Lord for only His grace can remove them.

Kim has two biological children, a son Jeremy, and a daughter Jamie. She also has one granddaughter Julia.

Kim is a cancer survivor and at the age of fifty-six has recently married an ordained minister that lost his wife Teresa to cancer; she went home to be with the Lord. She has also become a mother to her husband's and his late wife's four adopted grandchildren, A.J. who is twelve, Shaina who is eleven, Domenic who is ten and Mark who is nine

Kim will be the first to tell you that all of these things may not be considered gifts to most and in the past she also would not have seen her breast cancer or four young children at her age gifts. But she states now that they are nothing but gifts from the Lord as far as she is concerned. It is Kim's faith and relationship with Jesus that gives her the ability to be grateful on a daily basis, know matter what the day brings.

Kim resides in South Florida.